HE WILL GIVE YOU
Rest

HE WILL GIVE YOU

Rest

An Invitation and a Promise

RICHARD NEITZEL HOLZAPFEL
and GAYE STRATHEARN

DESERET
BOOK

SALT LAKE CITY, UTAH

Visit us at DeseretBook.com

Library of Congress Cataloging-in-Publication Data
Holzapfel, Richard Neitzel.
    He will give you rest : an invitation and a promise / Richard Neitzel Holzapfel and Gaye Strathearn.
        p. cm.
    Includes bibliographical references and index.
    ISBN 978-1-60641-667-9 (hardbound : alk. paper)
    1. Christian life—Mormon authors. 2. The Church of Jesus Christ of Latter-day Saints—Doctrines. I. Strathearn, Gaye. II. Title.
    BX8656.H658 2010
    248.4—dc22   2010011483

Printed in the United States of America
Quad/Graphics, Fairfield, PA

10 9 8 7 6 5 4 3 2

CONTENTS

ACKNOWLEDGMENTS

We appreciate Cherie Ardern, Jeni Broberg Holzapfel, Zachary Jacob Holzapfel, Ellen Kosmicki, Becky Low, and Lucy Strathearn for reading early drafts of chapters. Their comments and suggestions helped improve the content and raised some important questions that allowed us to further develop our thoughts on certain points.

We thank Joany Pinegar, administrative assistant at the Religious Studies Center, Brigham Young University, for her continued help, and our student research assistants Emily Broadbent, Alan Taylor Farnes, Berit Green, Chris Keneipp, Laurie Mildenhall, Rachael Moore, Kipp Muir, Vanessa Rothfels, and Alyne Tamir for their work with source checking.

Finally, we appreciate the support and interest of Deseret Book in this project and would especially like to thank Jana

Erickson, Suzanne Brady, Shauna Gibby, and Rachael Ward for their contributions.

Writing about a subject tends to clarify one's thoughts about it. That was certainly the case in this instance—we learned much and appreciated the opportunity to spend time with what has often been described as the most important invitation ever given to the human family: "Come unto me" (Matthew 11:28).

INTRODUCTION

*J*esus' invitation, "Come unto me, all ye that labour and are heavy laden," and his marvelous promise, "I will give you rest" (Matthew 11:28) are worthy of ongoing thoughtful consideration. President Henry B. Eyring said, "The words 'come unto Christ' are an invitation. It is the most important invitation you could ever offer to another person. It is the most important invitation anyone could accept."[1] Elder Jeffrey R. Holland explained, "The search for peace is one of the ultimate quests of the human soul. We all have highs and lows, but such times come and they usually always go. Kind neighbors assist. Beautiful sunshine brings encouragement. A good night's sleep usually works wonders. But there are times in all our lives when deep sorrow or suffering or fear or loneliness makes us cry out for the peace which only God Himself can bring. These are times of piercing spiritual hunger when even the dearest friends cannot fully come to our aid."[2] It is in such moments that Jesus' gracious invitation and comforting promise are needed most.

"Come unto me" is not the only invitation found in the book of Matthew. As New Testament scholar Mark Allan Powell noted, Matthew's Gospel "is a book of invitation, summoning the reader to seek God's kingdom and righteousness (6:33), to come to Jesus and experience rest (11:28), to hear his words and act on them (7:24), to understand the word and bear fruit (13:23), and to live a life of good works that brings glory to the Father in heaven (5:16)."[3]

It is important to note that Jesus' numerous invitations, including the one to come unto him, assume the operation of agency. There were those who did not accept Jesus' invitation then (19:16–22) and there are those who will not accept it today. The parable of the sower is a healthy reminder that there is a variety of soils—some that will bring forth fruits of the gospel and some that will not (13:3–8, 19–32).

Additionally, and more to the point for those who desire to be disciples, who want to be bound to Jesus Christ with his yoke (11:29–30), Jesus' invitation implies and assumes that we come to him completely. He expects more than simply bearing testimony: "I know God lives. I know Jesus is the Christ. I know Joseph Smith was a prophet of God. I know the Church is true." Although the affirmation of such important and consequential eternal truths is the foundation of our public witness and testimony, it is nevertheless only the confession of the "moment of

INTRODUCTION

recognition" that we have experienced in the conversion process.[4] Elder Dallin H. Oaks emphasizes this point: "To come unto Christ is not satisfied by a mere confession or declaration of belief in Him. It means to follow Him in order to become as He is."[5]

Nephi also challenged those who knew to take action: "Wherefore, do the things which I have told you I have seen that your Lord and your Redeemer should do; for, for this cause have they been shown unto me, that ye might know the gate by which ye should enter. For the gate by which ye should enter is repentance and baptism by water; and then cometh a remission of your sins by fire and by the Holy Ghost" (2 Nephi 31:17).

Even then, this is only the beginning of a spiritual journey to come fully unto Christ. Elder Bruce C. Hafen observed, "Receiving the Holy Ghost marks the *beginning* of our real spiritual growth, not the *end* of it. Baptism and the Holy Ghost only let us '[enter] in by the gate.'"[6] Nephi taught: "And now, my beloved brethren, after ye have gotten into this strait and narrow path, I would ask if all is done? Behold, I say unto you, Nay; for ye have not come thus far save it were by the word of Christ with unshaken faith in him, relying wholly upon the merits of him who is mighty to save. Wherefore, ye must press forward with a steadfastness in Christ" (31:19–20).

In Matthew 16, Jesus says, "If any man will come after me, let him deny himself, and take up his cross, and follow me" (v. 24). In Matthew 11, Jesus says simply and succinctly, "Take my yoke upon you, and learn of me" (v. 29). To come unto Jesus is to become a disciple of Christ—to "love the Lord thy God with all thine heart, and with all thy soul, and with all thy might" (Deuteronomy 6:5). Such dedication and commitment allow us to be "encircled about eternally in the arms of his love" (2 Nephi 1:15).

Elder Neil L. Andersen reflected: "The Lord's desire that we come unto Him and be wrapped in His arms is often an invitation to repent. 'Behold, he sendeth an invitation unto all men, for the arms of mercy are extended towards them, and he saith: Repent, and I will receive you' [Alma 5:33]. . . .

" . . . Divine forgiveness is one of the sweetest fruits of the gospel, removing guilt and pain from our hearts and replacing them with joy and peace of conscience. Jesus declares, 'Will ye not now return unto me, and repent of your sins, and be con-verted, that I may heal you?' [3 Nephi 9:13] . . .

"For most, repentance is more a journey than a one-time event. It is not easy. To change is difficult. It requires running into the wind, swimming upstream."[7]

Turning around and traveling only halfway toward Jesus will ultimately leave us emotionally, physically, and spiritually empty, even if it provides some worldly benefits now. Elder Neal A. Maxwell observed, "It is so easy to be halfhearted, but this only produces half the growth, half the blessings, and just half a life, really, with more bud than blossom."[8]

For various reasons and at different times in our lives we may choose to approach our Savior but keep our distance. Such a halfhearted disciple generally acknowledges that Jesus is the Christ—God's own Son—but hesitates to give himself or herself completely to him without reservation or precondition. Commenting on lukewarm disciples, German theologian and Christian martyr Dietrich Bonhoeffer noted: "He wants to follow, but feels obliged to insist on his own terms to the level of human understanding. The disciple places himself at the Master's disposal, but at the same time retains the right to dictate his own terms. But then discipleship is no longer discipleship, but a programme of our own to be arranged to suit ourselves, and to be judged in accordance with the standards of rational ethic."[9]

We may want to serve a mission but on our own terms and to a mission of our own choosing—or at least not to a certain mission the Lord may choose for us. We may desire to serve but only in the position and auxiliary of the Church where we feel most comfortable—unwilling to be, for a season, the "doorkeeper in the house of my God" (Psalm 84:10). This often means listening to and applying only certain teachings of those Jesus has sent—picking and choosing from general conference talks only those things we are anxious and willing to obey, while rejecting in our hearts those teachings that are troubling to our soul—those that demand a change in lifestyle and attitude.

In other cases, such halfhearted disciples want to be forgiven but refuse to forgive those for whom Jesus suffered in Gethsemane and died on Golgotha (D&C 64:9–10). They forget President Eyring's insight: "As we gather in that heavenly home, we will be surrounded by those who have been forgiven of all sin and who have forgiven each other."[10]

Sister Chieko N. Okazaki provides an analogy that helps

us understand what halfhearted discipleship looks like today: "I think we sometimes have the mistaken notion that religion is like a special room in our house. We go into this room when we need to 'do' religion. After all, we cook in the kitchen, we entertain in the living room, we wash in the bathroom, we sleep in the bedroom, and we 'do' religion in this spiritual room. The fallacy of this view of religious life is obvious. It means that we can walk out of that room and close the door behind us. . . . It also means that we spend most of our time in other rooms."[11]

Generally, one result of a halfhearted response to Jesus' invitation is never to receive all he offers in return for our obedience. We find ourselves attending church meetings, fulfilling our assignments, and regularly marking off the proverbial checklist, including having completed home/visiting teaching for the month, attended the temple, taught a nursery/priesthood/Relief Society class last Sunday, paid fast offerings and tithing, graduated from seminary, served a mission, and married in the temple. Yet we still carry heavy burdens and labor incessantly. We are often emotionally, spiritually, and physically exhausted despite all the signs of being active in the Church. Elder Maxwell noted, "One major cause of real fatigue, little appreciated by those so afflicted, is trying to serve two masters. This is devastating double duty."[12] Elder Hafen observes, "Some grind to a halt under the weight of overload and exhaustion. . . . We wouldn't lose momentum in these ways if more of us could live every day as truly consecrated disciples of Christ, rather than just being active in Church. Those who are well-intentioned but stuck in mere activity wonder why the joy of the journey has waned, perhaps without realizing that they have stopped growing spiritually. When the growth stops, so does the joy."[13]

Matthew remembered Jesus specifically inviting those who are weary and burdened. Certainly, given the historical and economic realities of the first century, in which most people struggled just to survive, this invitation to people who labored six days a week (Gentiles labored seven days a week) from morning to dusk throughout their lives must have been intriguing. Their heavy burdens were real—they lacked medical and dental care, they had no health or homeowners' insurance, and they had no retirement options, such as IRAs or employer-funded pensions or retirement contributions. They had a short life expectancy and experienced unfathomably high infant mortality rates, deadly diseases, and accidents in the home or work place that maimed significant numbers of people. It is likely that at any given time more than half the population was either sick or injured. Additionally, outside forces disrupted village life and travel—robbers, riots, and even wars, such as the Jewish Revolt from A.D. 66 to 70, which destroyed Jewish life in Judea and Galilee. The people also experienced various types of pressure and oppression from mounting taxes, tolls, and tributes gathered by the ruling elite—the Romans, their client kings, and absentee landlords. Finally, there were the additional burdens of sin, abandonment, divorce, childlessness, loneliness, and other heartaches common to our mortal existence, no matter when and where we live.

Jesus' consoling invitation still speaks to us today, even

though we live in a much different world from his original audience in rural Galilee—the possible origin of Matthew's Gospel—a world changed beyond recognition in many cases. For example, few people in western society worry about famine, starvation, and war in their own land; few expect to bury a child; few work from dawn to dusk seven or even six days a week for their entire lives. Many expect to retire from their employment and then to travel, garden, relax, and spend time with family, especially grandchildren. Employers generally compensate their employees for sick days, vacation days, and local and national holidays. The modern invention of the weekend provides another freedom from the ancient pattern of constant work.[14] Nevertheless, just as common people in the first century suffered from the traditions of the elders imposed on them by the Pharisees and other groups, so do we often carry other burdens, challenges, and problems imposed by modern society. These burdens of modern origin weigh us down and cause us to labor in our minds and hearts, if not in our bodies.

Interestingly, Jesus requires no prerequisites as we begin our journey to him. The invitation is in fact to those who labor and are heavy laden. President Boyd K. Packer astutely observes: "And so we appeal to all to come. . . . Come by families if you can, or alone if you must. . . . Many of you are burdened with unhappiness and worry and guilt. Many of you struggle under the bondage of degrading habits or wrestle with loneliness or disappointment and failure. Some of you suffer from broken homes, broken marriages, broken hearts. We are not offended at all of these things. All of these things may be set aside—overcome.

Whoever you are and whatever you are, we reach out to extend to you the hand of fellowship so that we can lift one another and lift others."[15]

The invitation continues to ring in our ears as we seek to escape the debilitating effects of a busy, complex, challenging world—a world that demands all our attention, not just our ears and eyes but also our very hearts and minds. This modern world, with the invention of electricity, has extended the length of our days so we can fill them up with more things to do—but not necessarily better things to do. Advances in such communications technology as cell phones, e-mails, and text messaging add to the demands of an increasingly intrusive world—it seems we can never escape, even for a moment. We are, after all, on call twenty-four hours a day, seven days a week.

We feel guilty if we do not answer the phone, respond to text messages or e-mails, or update our Facebook account. Today we are bombarded with technology and media (radios, iPods, TV, even movies on our computers), each clamoring for our attention and in some cases seeking to divert us from the path of consecrated discipleship. Almost every store, restaurant, and doctor's and dentist's office has music or a TV playing, often both at the same time. These competing sounds and images easily affect our mood, spirituality, and inner peace.

Added to these loud, daily distractions is an incessant economic expectation—an endless demand for new and fancier cars, bigger and better homes, larger and more expensive wardrobes, and toys of all kinds. Although there is nothing inherently wrong in possessing any of these things, seeking after them, especially when they pull us into a vortex of spiraling debt, eventually burdens us as much as the traditions of the elders did in the ancient world. Things never satisfy our eternal needs and only momentarily satisfy our worldly wants.

If many of us living in western society were to put everything we own in our front yard and compare it to what other people living around the world own, we would likely be astonished at the remarkable contrast. In modern western society we collect an amazing amount of stuff that takes time, room, and resources to own, store, protect, and use—a remarkable cost. Still, many of us, who already have sufficient for our needs, look at the man or woman living in a bigger house with more stuff than we have and feel deprived. We forget that in comparison to most people who have ever lived on earth, we are truly rich. Media highlights the super rich, and we then begin to compare ourselves with that infinitesimal fraction of the world's population. Sometimes, because we fail to see that we are already a blessed people, we fail to generously share our abundance because we say in our hearts that we do not have enough stuff yet!

President Spencer W. Kimball's call to greater discipleship through a generous fast offering still speaks to us today: "I think that when we are affluent, as many of us are, that we ought to be very, very generous . . . I think we should be very generous and give, instead of the amount we saved by our two meals of fasting, perhaps much, much more—ten times more where we are in a position to do it."[16] Some of us know people who have done exactly what President Kimball asked; they have given literally ten times more to the kingdom and other worthy causes. These affluent disciples share from their abundance in ways that would make many of us feel less consecrated. They are similar to those described in the Book of Mormon: "And they did impart of their substance, every man according to that which he had, to the poor, and the needy, and the sick, and the afflicted; and they did not wear costly apparel, yet they were neat and comely" (Alma 1:27). It is important to recognize that the Lord wants a people who are "neat and comely," a people who enjoy beauty, refinement, and the good things of the earth (D&C 59:16–20). The Lord does not require complete self-denial. He does not want us to live in a cave or in a desert place, rejecting all pleasures, comforts, and relationships, because self-denial is a form of selfishness—a focus on self instead of on Christ.

Created by the age of abundance, the pursuit of material possessions is furthered by the false notion that things can make us happy. Often, such expectations only increase our debt. Ironically, the new car or the new pair of running shoes soon loses its power to satisfy our immediate wants as we begin to focus on buying something else that we believe will make us happy, yet the debt remains and in many cases increases. We spend more than we earn, hoping all along to catch up someday.

All in all, we are weary in mind and body, and we carry heavy burdens—baggage of all kinds. Therefore, Jesus' promise "I will give you rest" is a spiritual lifeline for us. It is just as desirable and remarkable today as it was two thousand years ago. Yet what Jesus offers is more than the "rest" we can obtain by clearing the calendar. Anyone can do that! What Jesus promises is something more profound (John 14:27). This blessing itself comes through Jesus' infinite and eternal Atonement. Elder Tad R. Callister observed, "Among its many blessings, the Atonement brings peace. It not only cleanses us, but it consoles us."[17]

The invitation to come unto him and the attending promise "I will give you rest" is only part of what Jesus offers (Matthew 11:28). In what has been described as "some of the sweetest words ever attributed to Him—words that make intelligible Paul's appreciation for the 'meekness and gentleness of Christ' [2 Corinthians 10:1],"[18] Jesus says, "For I am meek and lowly in heart: and ye shall find rest unto your souls. For my yoke is easy, and my burden is light" (Matthew 11:29–30). At first this might seem incredibly contradictory: an easy yoke, a light burden! To understand what is meant, we need to consider: What is an easy yoke? What is a light burden? Exactly what kind of peace is Jesus offering? Can we truly obtain such promises? What does it mean to us today? How can we come unto Jesus more fully and completely so these blessings can be ours?

Sometimes identified as a "gospel reversal," the counterintuitive promises of an easy yoke and a light burden can also be described as a paradox. Terryl L. Givens notes that a "paradox—or tensions" only appear "to be logical contradictions."[19] Many New Testament scholars have noted that one of the strong themes in the scriptures is reversal.[20] Modern readers, as the original audience must have been themselves, are surprised, even shocked when Jesus says the meek, instead of the powerful, will inherit the earth (Matthew 5:5). In this regard, Elder Hafen identifies another paradox about Jesus' invitation to come unto him. He observes, "When we exert enough spiritual energy to move closer to the Savior, the good news is that He then moves closer to us, more than doubling our motion by joining it with His."[21] He also reminds us of the parable of the Father and two sons, the so-called parable of the prodigal son (Luke 15:11–32) and says, "I compare that father to Christ, who is so eager for our return that He comes to meet us and strengthens us all along our way . . . Christ's running to us is a vivid symbol of that grace. We talk often in the Church about coming to Christ. Perhaps we should talk more about how Christ also comes to us."[22]

So many more reversals are noted in the Gospels—they are found in Jesus' parables, teachings, and ministry. The most significant and greatest paradox is that the Savior and Redeemer died so that we could live (Mark 14:24).

Jesus' promise to us who "labour and are heavy laden" of a blessing of rest, an easy yoke, and a light burden might at first seem impossible. Yet, like other gospel paradoxes, the promises only appear to be contradictions. New Testament scholar A. E. Harvey reflected, "'I am meek and lowly in heart' (Matthew 11:29) defines 'the kind of king which Jesus was—one who comes to you in gentleness' (21:5), one who 'humbled himself' (Philippians 2:8). His kingship was so new, his rule such a reversal of the usual structures of authority, that his yoke had nothing to do with oppression. Paul, indeed, was to call it freedom."[23] In the end, Jesus, who knows the Father intimately and is willing to reveal him unto us so that we might enter into his rest, came to earth with power and authority as the divine Son of God. He will say to all those who come unto him, "Well done, thou good and faithful servant . . . enter thou into the joy of thy lord" (Matthew 25:21). Then will the obedient say, "For we which have believed do enter into rest" (Hebrews 4:3).

Chapter 1

JESUS' INVITATION
AND PROMISE

$\mathcal{O}$NE SCHOLAR OBSERVES THAT MATTHEW 11:25–30 RECORDS "perhaps the most important verses in the Synoptic Gospels."[1] More specifically, Elder James E. Talmage described verses 28–30 as "one of the grandest outpourings of spiritual emotion known to man."[2]

If these statements are true, then why is Matthew the only author to include this invitation: "Come unto me, all ye that labour and are heavy laden, and I will give you rest. Take my yoke upon you, and learn of me; for I am meek and lowly in heart: and ye shall find rest unto your souls. For my yoke is easy, and my burden is light"? (Matthew 11:28–30). Why was this teaching so important to Matthew? After all, Luke includes the three verses that precede them, in which Jesus speaks about knowing the Father (Luke 10:21–22); both Mark and Luke include the story that follows about plucking grain on the Sabbath (Mark 2:23–28; Luke 6:1–5).

Perhaps it has something to do with the fact that Matthew's Gospel was written to a Jewish audience and therefore emphasizes discipleship through works-righteousness—the things we must do to gain salvation. Matthew uses the Greek word for righteousness, *dikaiosynē*, seven times in his Gospel—five of them in the Sermon on the Mount; in contrast, Mark does not use the term at all, Luke uses it just once, and John uses it only twice (Matthew 3:15; 5:6, 10, 20; 6:1, 33; 21:32; Luke 1:75; John 16:8, 10).

It is therefore significant that in a Gospel where works-righteousness is so prominent, Matthew also includes an important counterbalance for those who feel the weight of such responsibility. The counterbalance expressed in Matthew 11:28–30 is just as important for modern readers as it was to Matthew's original audience in the first century. In fact, the importance of that counterbalance is reflected in the poetic form of the passage. Chiasmus, as Latter-day Saint scholar John W. Welch explains, "consists of arranging a series of words or ideas in one order, and then repeating this in reverse order." One of the important features of chiasmus is that "the main idea of the passage is placed at the turning point where the second half begins, which emphasizes it."[3] Matthew 11:28–30 can thus be formatted in the following way, with the ideas of laboring and being heavy laden paralleling the easy yoke and the light burden, and the two promises of rest paralleling each other.

1. Come unto me, all ye that labour and are heavy laden,
   2. and I will give you rest.
      3. Take my yoke upon you, and learn of me;
         for I am meek and lowly in heart;
   2. And ye shall find rest unto your souls.
1. For my yoke is easy, and my burden is light.[4]

At the turning point of this chiasmus is the invitation to take Jesus' yoke and learn about and from him. His yoke is not that of a tyrant, for he is meek and lowly in heart. He does not ask us to take his yoke so he can load additional burdens on us. Rather, he asks us to take his yoke because he loves us, because he wants to help us, because he wants us not just to endure mortality but to enter into a fulness of God's glory, both here and in the eternities.

To more fully appreciate the meaning of this text, we must examine it within the broader context of Matthew's Gospel and the more immediate context of the passages that surround it. As it stands in his Gospel, its immediate context is an important link between his discussion of knowing the Father and the Son (Matthew 11:25–27) and Jesus' proclamation that he is the Lord of the Sabbath (12:1–9).

Chapter 2

KNOWING THE FATHER

THE IMMEDIATE HISTORICAL CONTEXT OF JESUS' INVITATION and promise (Matthew 11:28–30) is found in the passages just before it (11:25–27) and just after it (12:1–14). We must therefore disregard the arbitrary chapter division between them. The chapter divisions and versifications in the King James Version of the Bible were added in 1560 to allow quick access to the text, but they sometimes interrupt a continuous narrative and destroy the natural flow of the story.[1] The three-part unit begins with a discussion of knowing the Father and ends with Jesus' declaration of authority over the Sabbath. Both are important in understanding Jesus' invitation and promise.

Matthew begins this critical unit with "At that time," signaling an important new chapter in his story (Matthew 12:1; see also Luke 10:21–22). He continues when Jesus prays, "I thank thee, O Father [Greek, *pater* (father)], Lord of heaven and earth" (Matthew 11:25). Many scholars agree that Jesus used the Aramaic address *abba*, a personal, even intimate way of praying to God. Jews did not address God with such familiar language. It should be remembered that Matthew wrote his Gospel in Greek, either translating Jesus' Aramaic words or using a Greek translation already in existence, making Matthew's Greek *pater* the equivalent of the Aramaic *abba* (see Mark 14:36 for such an attestation). Here Jesus addresses the Father in this way five times in three verses (11:25–27).

The Joseph Smith Translation provides another detail—Jesus is responding to the Father, who has called him. "**And** at that time **there came a voice out of heaven; and** Jesus answered and said, I thank thee, O Father, Lord of heaven and earth" (JST Matthew 11:25; JST changes in bold type).[2]

In this prayer, Jesus reveals his unique relationship with God. He knew God as his Father in a way no one else knew him or even claimed to have known him. The Gospels do not inform us when Jesus came to know the Father in this way; the scriptures reveal only hints (see, for example, Luke 2:49; D&C 93:12–13). There may have been a gradual unfolding of his special relationship with the Father, or there may have been one decisive revelatory moment, or a combination of both. But no matter how and when this special knowledge came to Jesus, the result was the same: he knew the Father in a way that no one else knew him. Jesus was uniquely alone in the world and different from every other person on the planet in this regard.

All of the studying, memorizing, and debating so typical of first-century efforts to understand the scriptures did not and could not help. The Gospels reveal that Jesus' knowledge of God did not come from learning about him through human effort or study. It should be remembered that Jesus most likely did not own a set of scriptures. Rather, he became familiar with the scriptures as other young Jewish children did—by hearing them read or recited by adults in the synagogue. Later, as he grew into young manhood, he had a chance to read from the sacred scrolls on the Sabbath in the synagogue in Nazareth (Luke 4:16). That he knew them well is revealed in several passages (Matthew 12:3, 5; 19:4; 21:16; 42; 22:31).

There may certainly have been specific passages that resonated with Jesus—passages that acted as catalysts in his growing self-awareness—but his knowledge came from an awareness of the Father's presence that only he had because he was without sin. It came from listening carefully to the Father's voice as it came to him; observing the Father perform his work in the world; and finally, by doing what he saw the Father do. In other words, Jesus knew the Father from personal experience.

Such intimacy has a parallel in human relationships. Perhaps you have attended the funeral of someone you assumed you knew well, only to be surprised to hear a son or a daughter reveal some things that you never knew about that person—details and insights that could be known only through a close family association. That is precisely what Jesus is doing here: announcing things that only the Son could know about the Father.

21

In another important Gospel paradox, Jesus further informed his listeners that the Father had hid the truth from the "wise and prudent [Greek, *synetoi*, learned]" and had instead revealed them to babes [Greek, *nēpioi*, innocent people]," a reference to his un-sophisticated disciples (11:25; see also 18:3–4, 6, 10; 25:40, 45).

The burst of praise continues when Jesus prays, "Even so, Father: for so it seemed good in thy sight. All things are deliv-ered unto me of my Father: and no man knoweth the Son, but the Father; neither knoweth any man the Father, save the Son, and he to whomsoever the Son will reveal him" (11:26–27). In what has been described as "one of the most crucial passages for understanding the character of this Gospel and its presenta-tion of Jesus," Jesus says that his Father has revealed himself di-rectly to Jesus. He discovered the Father not through study but through his special relationship with the Father—Jesus is his Son.[3] Apparently, "Jesus uses a proverb readily understandable by Mediterraneans who believe 'Like father, like son.'"[4] This chiastic parallelism of the two lines could also be read, "only father and son really know each other."[5] Additionally, Jesus states that any-one wanting to know the Father can do so only through the Son. This constitutes an exclusive, unrestricted, and absolute claim of authority, even audacious in its proclamation. From the Pharisees' point of view, this was pure blasphemy, and it is therefore not surprising that they wanted Jesus dead (12:14).

The Joseph Smith Translation adds another important in-sight: "All things are delivered unto me of my Father: and no man knoweth the Son, but the Father; neither knoweth any man the Father, save the Son, and to whom the Son will reveal himself, they shall see the Father also" (JST Matthew 11:27).

In light of Jesus' declaration about coming to know God, what is to be done? If Jesus is the only one who can reveal the Father to us, what are we to do? Jesus answers these questions when he issues "what is still the most welcoming and encouraging invitation ever offered. 'Come to me,' he said, 'and I'll give you rest' [see Matthew 11:28]."[6] He adds, "Learn of me" (11:29). We discover further depth of meaning in "learn of me" when we consider that the phrase can also mean "learn from me," or "learn about me" (see chapter 4, "A Call to Discipleship").

We will come to know the Father when we accept Jesus' invitation. As we will see, knowing the Son is an important aspect of coming to know the Father and entering into his rest (D&C 84:24).

Chapter 3

JESUS' AUTHORITY

*A*FTER MATTHEW RECORDS JESUS' LOVING INVITATION (Matthew 11:28–30), he tells the story of a Sabbath day when Jesus and his disciples walk through a field (12:1–9; see also Mark 2:23–28; Luke 6:1–5). The placement of the chapter division at the beginning of Matthew 12:1 is regrettable, because this is actually not a new story, and the chapter division compromises its natural flow.[1]

The telling of the Sabbath day story immediately following the announcement of the special blessing that will come to those who accept Jesus' invitation is to demonstrate how his offer to give us peace and to lighten our burdens works in a real-life situation. It also reveals why we should accept Jesus' invitation to come unto him and to learn of him. Finally, it tells us why we can rely on Jesus and trust that he is able to fulfill the promise he has so graciously offered.

Matthew states, "At that time Jesus went on the sabbath day through the corn; and his disciples were an hungred, and began to pluck the ears of corn, and to eat" (12:1). The 1611 King James Version word *corn* means not "maize" but "grain." Maize was taken to the Old World only after it was discovered in the Americas. Traditionally, wheat and barley were the principal grains grown in the ancient Near East; they were an important source of protein. We should therefore picture in our minds the disciples walking along a grain field on their way to another village where Jesus will preach, teach, and heal (12:9–13).

The combination of Sabbath day, grain field, hungry disciples, and Jesus should immediately point our attention to a Sabbath day controversy—a major point of contention between Jesus and his enemies throughout his ministry. And that is exactly what happens: "But when the Pharisees saw it, they said unto him, Behold, thy disciples do that which is not lawful to do upon the sabbath day" (12:2). The Pharisees play an important role at the beginning of this story as Jesus and his disciples walk by a grain field and at the end of the synagogue scene (12:14).

For many Jews, the Sabbath day was an important boundary marker—its observance separated Israel from their Gentile neighbors. Proper observance was the subject of one of the commands found in the Decalogue recorded in the Torah (Exodus 20:8–11; Deuteronomy 5:12–15). Notice that no other directive is discussed in more detail than the Sabbath in the Ten

Commandments. Additionally, the Sabbath was blessed at the end of Creation itself: "And on the seventh day God ended his work which he had made; and he rested on the seventh day from all his work which he had made. And God blessed the seventh day, and sanctified it: because that in it he had rested from all his work which God created and made" (Genesis 2:2–3). This only enhanced the significance of the Sabbath day for Jews living during the first century A.D.

Strict Jewish observance of the Sabbath was well known, legendary in fact, and during times of persecution many Jews chose to willingly die rather than violate the Sabbath. For example, when Antiochus IV (175–163 B.C.) became the ruler of the Seleucid Empire he attempted to consolidate his power against the growing influence of the Romans in the west, the Parthians on the east, and the Ptolemies (Egypt) in the south.[2] Eventually he decided that complete Hellenization, making his world Greek in every way—language, religion, and culture—would unify his kingdom against the forces threatening the stability of his regime. However, the Jews living within the political boundaries of the Seleucid Empire refused to obey. Eventually, Antiochus outlawed the practice of Judaism, killing those who refused to become Greek. Numerous men and women remained faithful to the Lord, the Torah, and the Sabbath day (1 and 2 Maccabees in the Apocrypha).[3]

From the end of the Old Testament period until the coming of John the Baptist, the Jews were without a prophetic voice. As a result, various voices "claimed authority to interpret the Law.

For example, the Samaritans ultimately rejected the Jerusalem temple and priesthood and therefore the priests' right to interpret the Law. . . . Later, the Essenes also discredited the temple and the priests in Jerusalem and offered alternative interpretations of the Law. . . . In addition, the cadre of scribes that grew up, either because of priests' disinterest in the Law or because the scribes disagreed with priests' interpretations, became a formidable force for understanding the Law chiefly in a Pharisaic way."[4] In this historical context Jewish leaders debated the Law, including what was appropriate Sabbath behavior in order to protect the Sabbath day. In an effort to provide specific rules for Torah observance (beyond what the Bible outlined), Jewish leaders, wise men, sages, and alternative voices developed a significant body of tradition to guide behavior, including Sabbath day observance.

The rabbis eventually "went on to classify 39 kinds of work as forbidden . . . including reaping."[5] The traditions of the elders were, "according to rabbinic tradition, the oral law (*torah she-be-'al peh*) . . . given together with the written law [found in the five books of Moses]."[6] Eventually, written down sometime in the end of the second century A.D., the Mishnah is the classical repository of the oral law handed down through time. Not all Jews accepted these traditions of the elders. For example, the Sadducees rejected much of the Pharisees' oral law.[7] The Essenes, those people who wrote or collected the Dead Sea Scrolls, had another system of oral law that diverged rather dramatically from the Pharisees' interpretations of the law.[8]

New Testament scholar A. E. Harvey observed, "With all

their efforts to make the Law fully applicable to present-day conditions they had only succeeded in making the yoke more oppressive."[9]

Jesus rejected these commandments of men, the traditions of the elders (Matthew 15:1–20). He taught that instead of protecting the Sabbath, these man-made rules often added unnecessary burdens to the common people. Further, Jesus believed that some of the regulations established by the elders actually circumvented the original intent of the commandment, "making the word of God of none effect through your tradition, which ye have delivered: and many such like things do ye" (Mark 7:13).

In the first story in Matthew 12, Jesus declares the disciples "guiltless," indicating that he rejected the Pharisees' interpretation of Sabbath day observance and citing his authority to do so as "Lord even of the sabbath day" (12:7–8). The Law itself provided opportunities for "strangers" and the "poor" to pluck grain in fields that did not belong to them (Deuteronomy 23:24–25; cf. Leviticus 19:9; 23:22). Therefore, the issue in this instance was whether or not such activity constituted a Sabbath day violation.

In this case Jesus cites a precedent for overriding, superseding, or suspending a Torah commandment in order to satisfy hunger: "But he said unto them, Have ye not read what David did, when he was an hungred, and they that were with him; how he entered into the house of God, and did eat the shewbread, which was not lawful for him to eat, neither for them which were with him, but only for the priests? [1 Samuel 21:3–6] Or have ye not read in the law, how that on the sabbath days the priests in the temple profane the sabbath [Numbers 28:9–11], and are blameless?" (Matthew 12:3–5).

As this story points out, Jesus believed it was possible to know the scriptures without truly understanding them. Even Satan could quote chapter and verse (Matthew 4:5–6). In this case, his enemies may have had an academic understanding of the scriptures, but Jesus says they did not understand their true meaning (see also Matthew 17:10; 19:7; 21:42). However, the main point of the story is not Jesus' exegetical skills (his ability to provide a nuanced interpretation of the scriptures) but his personal authority: *"But I say unto you,* That in this place is one greater than the temple. But if ye had known what this meaneth, I will have mercy, and not sacrifice, ye would not have condemned the guiltless. For the Son of man is Lord even of the sabbath day"* (Matthew 12:6–8; emphasis added). Certainly Jesus saw himself in ways that no other person did—his self-understanding provided him confidence that he alone understood God's will and, as his agent, acted as his Father would act.

As the Lord of the Sabbath, Jesus challenged the Pharisees to observe the intent of the law; and in this particular case, the intent of the law was mercy. In an economy based on slavery, servitude, and hard work, the Sabbath provided freedom from labor one day each week. The Torah principle that allowed the poor to pluck grain from a landholder's field also demonstrated God's mercy as he provided the stranger and the poor with food to eat. Combined, the Sabbath and plucking grain provided true rest, that is, freedom from work and freedom from hunger.

In this story, Jesus argues that *if* David could violate the Torah principles to satisfy legitimate human needs, *then* he, Jesus, as the Son of David—one greater than David—had the right and authority to do the same. It is worth noting that David had already been anointed king (1 Samuel 16:13), though he was not yet enthroned in Jerusalem at the time of this incident; likewise, Jesus had been anointed (Acts 10:38), though not yet enthroned on the right hand of the Father. Further, because he knew the Father (Matthew 11:27) and had been appointed Lord of the Sabbath, Jesus alone was qualified to determine what constituted appropriate observance.

Jesus and his disciples then left the field and went into the synagogue (Matthew 12:9; Mark 3:1–6; Luke 6:6–11). We know from several independent sources that it was Jesus' custom to worship, teach, and preach in the Jewish synagogues in Galilee, which were the primary religious sites away from the temple in Jerusalem (Luke 4:16). On this particular Sabbath day, Jesus encountered in the synagogue "a man which had his hand withered" (Matthew 12:10).

Some Pharisees, presumably visiting from Jerusalem to obtain firsthand information about the teacher from Nazareth, were present, "And they asked him, saying, Is it lawful to heal on the sabbath days?" (12:10). Matthew reveals, however, that they were not interested in learning from him, as Jesus had earlier invited (11:28–30). Instead, they asked the question so "that they might accuse him" (12:10).

As with plucking grain on the Sabbath, healing on the

Sabbath was one of the points debated in first-century Judaism. Some believed that emergency needs, such as delivering a baby or the imminent danger of someone losing his life, called for the suspension of Sabbath observance to assist the individuals. Others believed that treatment for a sickness or injury that was not life threatening should be delayed until the Sabbath ended.

In this context of debate and interpretation, Jesus, as was often his practice, responds to his questioners by asking a counter question: "And he said unto them, What man shall there be among you, that shall have one sheep, and if it fall into a pit on the sabbath day, will he not lay hold on it, and lift it out?" (12:11). Apparently, most Jews would have agreed with Jesus' interpretation. Jesus asks further, "How much then is a man better than a sheep?" (12:12). Clearly, Jesus prioritizes his concerns— men, women, and children hold a special place in Jesus' plan to save the cosmos.

Jesus then states the fundamental truth about the Sabbath day: it was a day to do good (12:12). To demonstrate his authority to both interpret the law and to heal those with heavy burdens, Jesus says to the man, "Stretch forth thine hand. And he stretched it forth; and it was restored whole, like as the other" (12:13).

Neither story (the plucking of grain nor the healing in the synagogue) suggests that Jesus wanted people to abandon or abolish appropriate Sabbath observance. Jesus defines the special day as one set apart, a special day, a restorative gift to humans from a loving Creator. The question was not whether one should observe

JESUS' AUTHORITY

the Sabbath day but rather *how* one should observe it. Jesus came, as Isaiah prophesied, to free people from human yokes and man-made commandments: "The Spirit of the Lord God is upon me; because the Lord hath anointed me to preach good tidings unto the meek; he hath sent me to bind up the brokenhearted, to proclaim liberty to the captives, and the opening of the prison to them that are bound; to proclaim the acceptable year of the Lord" (Isaiah 61:1–2).

Those who first heard Matthew's Gospel read or who heard this story told, even by an eyewitness, would have immediately recalled Jesus' invitation to come unto him and to learn from him. By learning the will of God, in this instance his intent for Sabbath observance, one throws off the heavy yokes carved by human hands and replaces them with those lovingly made by God—an easy yoke. Doing so will immediately lighten our burdens and give us rest here and now. Finally, since the Father has given the Son all authority (Matthew 11:27; cf. 9:6; 28:18), Jesus is not only willing but able to reveal the Father, as promised in Matthew 11:25–27, and thereby reveal God's will concerning the Sabbath day.

Today, we do not expect a group of Pharisees to come from Jerusalem to see if we are observing the traditions of the elders. Instead, modern society and popular culture have created a new set of traditions, obligations, and expectations that can weigh us down. These include the pursuit of perpetual youth and the never-ending need to be popular, admired, and envied. They also include the need to conform to political correctness—to accept what society declares right instead of allowing people to vote their conscience. Diversity, a much-touted slogan, is unacceptable when it diverges from what popular culture accepts and promotes. As a result, society points a proverbial finger and attempts to shame, belittle, challenge, pressure, and condemn us for the way we live, adding to our burdens the weight of public disapproval just as heavy as the Pharisees' self-righteous condemnation of Jesus in these stories.

On a basic level, the commandments of men or traditions of the elders include the pressure to live in the right neighborhood, to drive the right car, and to own the right wardrobe. Elder Bruce C. Hafen captured the essence of the spirit of our times when he wrote: "Every day we hear messages of indulgence from today's culture of self-absorption and personal entitlement: you are entitled to a life of pleasure; go ahead, pamper yourself—you deserve it."[10]

Our children and grandchildren have a double burden. Not only have they inherited Western attitudes about unrestricted consumption—"He who has the most toys wins!"—but they have also failed to learn the lessons from the generations who lived through the Great Depression and World War II—"Use it up, wear it out, make it do, or do without."

Voices from a variety of sources, including TV, the Internet, current movies, modern music, and popular magazines, seek our notice. Not only do modern-day Pharisees want the attention of our eyes and ears but they want our hearts and minds as well. They want to shape our attitudes and control our lifestyle in ways much more insidious and burdensome than the strictures the oral Torah placed around the Law two thousand years ago. These heavy burdens and human-constructed yokes weigh us down and burn us out. In the story of the Sabbath day, Matthew provides an example of how Jesus lightens the burdens that come as a result of taking upon us the false traditions and values of our age—freeing us to live out God's original will.

Chapter 4

A CALL TO DISCIPLESHIP

IN ADDITION TO UNDERSTANDING THE IMMEDIATE CONTEXT surrounding Matthew 11:28–30, it is also important to see how these verses fit in the larger themes of Matthew's Gospel. One Matthean theme that is particularly important is discipleship. Our passage picks up this theme in a number of ways, although they are not always easily recognized in our present English translation. Before we can recognize and appreciate these connections, however, we must discuss the concept of discipleship in general.

Matthew's Gospel has been described as "a manual on discipleship."[1] Thematically, there are two ways in which discipleship is emphasized. First, Matthew's Gospel includes five major discourses: the Sermon on the Mount (5–7), the apostolic commission (10), the parables discourse (13), the community/church discourse (18), and the apocalyptic discourse (24–25). We know that these discourses are a conscious literary device because at the end of each one Matthew includes a statement such as "when Jesus had ended these sayings" (7:28; see also 11:1; 13:53; 19:1). After the final discourse he concludes, "And it came to pass, when Jesus had finished *all these sayings* . . ." (26:1; emphasis added). Significantly, all five of these discourses are specifically directed to his disciples.[2] Therefore it can be safely assumed that an important purpose of each discourse is to teach about discipleship.

Second, the last direction Jesus gives to the eleven disciples before ascending into heaven is, "Go ye therefore, and teach all nations" (28:19). Normally Matthew uses the Greek word *didaskō* to indicate teaching in general.[3] In fact, this is the word he uses in verse 20: "Teaching them to observe all things whatsoever I have commanded you." But in verse 19, Matthew makes a distinction. Jesus' commission is not merely directing the disciples to teach people about the gospel; there is no salvation in knowing about baptism or knowing about the commandments. Rather, his commission is to teach all nations so that they are willing to pay the price to become a disciple. Therefore, in this instance, instead of using the verb *didaskō*, Matthew uses *mathēteuō*, which literally means to "make disciples." The nuance of this Greek verb indicates that Jesus commissions the disciples to "Go ye therefore, and teach [make disciples of] all nations" (Matthew 28:19). That this is the last direction Jesus gives to his disciples in Matthew's Gospel indicates the importance of discipleship throughout the text.

Discipleship is an important theme throughout the New Testament Gospels, particularly in Matthew. The Greek word translated "disciple" in the New Testament is *mathētēs*, which basically means "a student." In the first century the relationship between disciple and master was not a casual association but one of deep commitment and loyalty. Sometimes a disciple is described as an apprentice, which emphasizes not only the responsibility of the master but also the formal indenture of the disciple to the master. Discipleship, therefore, denotes a strong association of commitment. Thus the use of the word *disciple* in the New Testament often makes a distinction from the members of the crowds that followed Jesus. Disciples certainly were followers of Christ, but the people in the crowds who followed Jesus are not usually identified as disciples. Those who made up the crowd followed Jesus after he taught the Sermon on the Mount (8:1), they followed him seeking to be healed (12:15; 14:13–14; 20:30–34; John 6:2), and they sought after him because he fed them (John 6:26), but there is no indication that the commitment of these individuals lasted any longer than the immediate circumstance. In other words, their interest in Jesus generally did not rise to the level of discipleship.

Commitment to discipleship usually comes at a cost. Although Jesus is often portrayed with open arms welcoming all into his circle, he also makes some very pointed statements about the price of discipleship. Because these sayings are scattered throughout the Gospels, it is easy for the casual reader to overlook them or miss their significance, but it is important that modern readers also recognize this nuance of Jesus' teachings. To highlight some of these teachings, we will briefly discuss just four passages.

At the conclusion of his Sermon on the Mount, Jesus declared, "Not every one that saith unto me Lord, Lord, shall enter into the kingdom of heaven; but he that doeth the will of my Father which is in heaven. Many will say to me in that day, Lord, Lord, have we not prophesied in thy name? and in thy name have cast out devils? and in thy name done many wonderful works? And then will I profess unto them, I never knew you" (Matthew 7:21–23). The Joseph Smith Translation pointedly changes the phrase "I never knew you" to "**Ye** never knew **me**" (JST changes in bold type).

Although declarations of testimony and good works are always important parts of discipleship, in and of themselves they are not sufficient. Ultimately, Christian discipleship is about cultivating a relationship and having a deep connection with both God the Father and with his Son. In the Great Intercessory Prayer, Jesus prayed, "And this is life eternal, that they might know thee the only true God, and Jesus Christ, whom thou hast sent" (John 17:3). But the idea is not just that we know about them; it is about knowing them from personal experience.

Peter taught this important principle in his discussion of the ladder to perfection in 2 Peter 1, although it is difficult to see the distinction in our English translation. Peter uses two related words that are both translated as knowledge: *gnōsis* and *epignōsis*. He seems to be using *gnōsis* to refer to vicarious knowledge; for example, knowledge that can come from reading a book, watching television, or hearing a lecture. This is an important element of discipleship. In contrast, Peter uses *epignōsis* to refer to experiential knowledge. He indicates the purpose of this ladder to perfection: "Wherefore the rather, brethren, give diligence to make your calling and election sure: for if ye do these things, ye shall never fall" (2 Peter 1:10). For an individual to receive his or her calling and election they must give "all diligence, add to your faith virtue; and to virtue knowledge (*gnōsis*); and to knowledge (*gnōsis*) temperance; and to temperance patience; and to patience godliness; and to godliness brotherly kindness; and to brotherly kindness charity. For if these things be in you, and abound, they make you that ye shall neither be barren nor unfruitful in the knowledge (*epignōsis*) of our Lord Jesus Christ" (1:5–8). Note that vicarious knowledge is the third rung on this ladder. It is an essential part of the journey: we must know about Christ because it is essential to continue the journey, but it is not the destination. Only when we have completed all of the rungs and experienced the pure love of Christ, charity, will we have *epignōsis* of Jesus and truly be his disciple. This process does not happen overnight; it takes time, but it is an important difference between the person who thinks he has earned the right to enter the kingdom of heaven, and the one who does the will of the Father. Joseph Smith Translation Matthew 7:23 suggests that the Father's will, and the prerequisite to entering the kingdom, is to know the Son. It is conceivable that those who thought they were eligible for the kingdom knew about the Son, but discipleship is about knowing him through experience.

In a second passage Jesus teaches that the path of discipleship results in significant trials and tribulations: "And a certain scribe came, and said unto him, Master, I will follow thee whithersoever thou goest. And Jesus saith unto him, The foxes have holes, and the birds of the air have nests; but the Son of man hath not where to lay his head. And another of his disciples said unto him, Lord, suffer me first to go and bury my father. But Jesus said unto him, Follow me; and let the dead bury their dead" (Matthew 8:19–22). In Matthew's Gospel these discipleship verses are used differently than they are in Luke's Gospel. In fact, they seem a little out of place in a chapter where Matthew has gathered together a series of miracles. But they are here for a reason: to introduce the miracle of the stilling of the storm (8:23–27).

In Matthew's version, the miracle is not told just to show that Jesus has power over the wind and the waves, though that seems to be the purpose in Mark and Luke's renditions. For Matthew the point of the story is Jesus' emphasis on the faith of the disciples or, more precisely, the lack thereof. In his account, the first thing Jesus does when his disciples wake him from his sleep is to comment on their lack of faith: "Why are ye fearful, O ye of little faith?" (Matthew 8:26). Only then does he rebuke the winds and the sea. This is the reverse of the order in Mark and Luke. Matthew is not only showing that there is a cost to *becoming* a disciple—not having the security/safety/comforts of a home and, at times, having to put love of God above even love of family

(8:18–22)—but also teaching us that once we make that commitment and enter into the boat (or the Church), trials and tribulations will continue to buffet us.[4] In other words, while a person in the crowd may walk away when life becomes hard, a disciple does not. Instead of fraying the bonds of discipleship, trials and tribulation serve to strengthen them.

A third Matthean passage brings together and reiterates the aspects of discipleship taught in the previous two passages. At Caesarea Philippi, Jesus asks the question, "Whom do men say that I the Son of man am?" They reply, "Some say that thou art John the Baptist: some, Elias; and others, Jeremias, or one of the prophets." Then Jesus turns to the disciples and asks, "But whom say ye that I am?" Peter then makes his famous declaration, "Thou art the Christ, the Son of the living God." To which Jesus responds, "Blessed art thou, Simon Bar-jona: for flesh and blood hath not revealed it unto thee, but my Father which is in heaven" (16:13–17). Peter knows who Jesus is because of revelation from the Father. Almost immediately after this experience Jesus taught his disciples that he must go to Jerusalem where he would "suffer many things of the elders and chief priests and scribes, and be killed, and be raised again the third day." Peter, in contrast to his earlier declaration about Jesus' messianic status, "began to rebuke [Jesus], saying, Be it far from thee, Lord: this shall not be unto thee" (16:21–22). Peter's response suggests that he saw an incongruity between Jesus being the Messiah and having to submit himself to the power of others.

It is in this context that Jesus teaches the Twelve about the costs of choosing to follow him. "Then said Jesus unto his disciples, If any man will come after me, let him deny himself, and take up his cross, and follow me" (16:24). Following Jesus as a disciple means following him not just when it is convenient, and not just when we can see the immediate tangible benefits, but also when following him means persecution, denial of comforts, and even death. The Joseph Smith Translation adds, "And now for a man to take up his cross, is to deny himself all ungodliness, and every worldly lust, and keep my commandments" (JST Matthew 16:26). In commenting on Matthew 6:24, two scholars have noted, "Our text drives home the point that the disciples—and implicitly, all believers—must not passively observe their Lord and what he does. They are not to be seated spectators watching from the grandstand . . . Rather must they themselves enter the arena after their Lord . . . Jesus is not a substitute but a leader. He does not do something for those who do nothing. Instead he commands, 'Follow me.' . . . This authoritative call leaves no room for considerations of convenience or even self-preservation. Discipleship is a doing of what is right, no matter how irksome the privations, no matter how great the dangers."[5] Disciples are not "seated spectators watching from the grandstand." Disciples are those who are actively engaged in the cause of building the kingdom, even when it is inconvenient or difficult or painful. That is part of the cost of discipleship.

Perhaps even more pointed than these Matthean passages are Jesus' discipleship sayings recorded in Luke 14: "And there went great multitudes with him: and he turned, and said unto them, If any man come to me, and hate not his father, and mother, and wife, and children, and brethren, and sisters, yea, and his own life also, he cannot be my disciple. And whosoever doth not bear his cross, and come after me, cannot be my disciple. For which of you, intending to build a tower, sitteth not down first, and counteth the cost, whether he have sufficient to finish it? Lest haply, after he hath laid the foundation, and is not able to finish it, all that behold it begin to mock him, saying, This man began to build, and was not able to finish. Or what king, going to make war against another king, sitteth not down first, and consulteth whether he be able with ten thousand to meet him that cometh against him with twenty thousand? Or else, while the other is yet a great way off, he sendeth an ambassage, and desireth conditions of peace. So likewise, whosoever he be of you that forsaketh not all that he hath, he cannot be my disciple" (Luke 14:25–33).

Verse 26 is a prickly verse. A person cannot be a disciple unless they "hate" their family? Is that really what Jesus taught? How can we reconcile this saying with teachings that families can be eternal? There is no doubt that Jesus uses hyperbole here to capture his audience's attention. He is not advocating that people generally should hate their family; rather, he uses the family as a symbol for that which is most precious to us and thus teaches that being a disciple is not just about consecrating peripheral aspects of our lives to God but also consecrating those things that are most important to us. In a sense, this verse is the Christian equivalent of the Mosaic injunction to bring animals without blemish to the altar of the temple. Being a disciple is about not letting

45

our focus be distracted from the things of eternal significance; our most important focus must be our love of and commitment to God. Everything else (even the second great commandment) is ancillary to the first commandment to love God with "all of thy heart, and with all thy soul, and with all thy mind" (Matthew 22:37).

Likewise, if people are not willing to take up their cross and come after Jesus, they cannot be his disciple. The Joseph Smith Translation interprets the phrase "take up his cross" as a commitment to living the commandments: "And now for a man to take up his cross, is to deny himself all ungodliness, and every worldly lust, and keep my commandments" (Matthew 16:24, note d). Luke 14:28 in the Joseph Smith Translation of Luke adds: "Wherefore, settle this in your hearts, that ye will do the things which I shall teach and command you." The two parables that follow this passage (about preparing to build a house and going into battle) reinforce for us the idea that the commitment of discipleship does not come passively or by chance; it must be a conscious decision, and it is something concerning which we must sit down and consider the cost. Each of these parables speaks to the importance of an individual understanding the requirements that Jesus expects from those who would be his disciples. Thus, discipleship is not easy, convenient, or automatic. President James E. Faust taught, "Most of us think that the price of discipleship is too costly and too burdensome. For many it involves the giving up of too much. But the cross is not as heavy as it appears to be."[6]

In Matthew 11:28–30, Jesus does not mention the words

disciple or *discipleship*. Nevertheless, it is clear that this passage must be understood within this context. Even without the use of the technical terms the passage is linked to the larger discussion of discipleship in Matthew in two key ways. First, we have already noted the Greek word for disciple is *mathētēs*. When Jesus says, "Take my yoke upon you, and learn of me" (11:29), he is issuing a call to discipleship because he uses the Greek verb "to learn" (*manthanō*, which comes from the same Greek stem as *mathētēs* and *mathēteuō*). In using *manthanō*, Jesus emphasizes the responsibility of disciples in the learning process. It is important to recognize that this call Jesus extends is not a casual invitation; rather, the verb form is an imperative, indicating that Jesus commands it. We are commanded to learn of Jesus.

In addition, while the King James translators rendered the phrase as "learn of me," it can also be understood to be "learn from me." Thus Jesus is not just asking people to learn about him but is inviting them to become disciples and commanding them to learn from him, learn what he has to teach, learn how to know the Father. After all, that is what a disciple does: learns from the master teacher.

Second, Jesus' invitation to "come" (Greek, *deute*) is frequently used as a call to discipleship, which is sometimes accepted and sometimes rejected. For example, Jesus invited Peter, Andrew, and by implication, James and John to come (*deute*) follow me and I will make you fishers of men (Matthew 4:19; author's translation). Their immediate acceptance showed their willingness to embark on a new life. In describing this story,

Matthew's mention of the fishing boats, nets, and Zebedee, James and John's father, are not just side notes. Rather, Zebedee stands as a symbol for the power that gave James and John their mortal life, and the boats and the fishing nets act as symbols for the power that sustains their mortal life. Their call to leave these behind was a call to a life of discipleship following the lead of their master—a life that would involve a different and heavier set of responsibilities and priorities. Matthew teaches that their responsibility as disciples/apostles is to do the things that Jesus does, and in Matthew that is specifically to heal the sick and preach the good news (4:23; 9:35; 11:4–5). Thus as Jesus extends their apostolic call he charges them to preach: "The kingdom of heaven is at hand. Heal the sick, cleanse the lepers, raise the dead, [and] cast out devils" (10:7–8). The call to follow Jesus was, first and foremost, a call to minister to others.

Not everyone, however, was willing to leave everything behind and respond to the Savior. For some the costs of discipleship were more than they were willing to sacrifice. The immediate response of Peter, Andrew, James, and John is in stark contrast to that of the rich young man (and the house of Israel) that we see later in the Gospel. Jesus extended the same invitation to the rich young man to "come (*deuro*) and follow me."[7] This time, however, the invitation was declined because "he had great possessions," which he was unwilling to give up (19:21–22). Likewise, in the parable of the marriage of the king's son, the king who symbolizes God invites his covenant people to come to the wedding and participate in celebrations of the kingdom of heaven:

"Behold, I have prepared my dinner: my oxen and my fatlings are killed, and all things are ready: come (*deute*) unto the marriage" (22:4). But the covenant people, who were first invited, also declined the invitation: "But they made light of it, and went their ways, one to his farm, another to his merchandise" (22:5).

Although Matthew 11:28–30 must be understood in the greater context of discipleship, it is also instructional to recognize the unique aspects of discipleship embedded in this invitation. It is here that we see some of the paradox of Jesus' teachings about discipleship, particularly in relation to his teachings about the cost of discipleship. For instance, instead of inviting his audience to "Come, follow me" (Luke 18:22), in this instance Jesus invites them to "Come unto me" (Matthew 11:28). This was the same invitation that Jesus repeatedly extended when he came to the New World as recorded in 3 Nephi 11. In fact, it is one of the major differences between Matthew's Sermon on the Mount and its Book of Mormon counterpart. "Blessed are the poor in spirit who come unto me, for theirs is the kingdom of heaven" (3 Nephi 12:3; cf. Matthew 5:3). "And behold, I have given you the law and the commandments of my Father, that ye shall believe in me, and that ye shall repent of your sins, and come unto me with a broken heart and a contrite spirit. Behold, ye have the commandments before you, and the law is fulfilled. Therefore come unto me and be ye saved" (3 Nephi 12:19–20; cf. Matthew 5:19–20). "Therefore, if ye shall come unto me, or shall desire to come unto me, and rememberest that thy brother hath aught against thee—Go thy way unto thy brother, and first be reconciled to thy brother, and then come unto me with full purpose of heart, and I will receive you" (3 Nephi 12:23–24; cf. Matthew 5:23–24).

Note that the invitation to "come" in Matthew 11:28 and 3 Nephi is not a call to minister to others by preaching and healing, as we discussed above. Rather, it is an invitation to "come unto him." The implication is that he invites them to come unto him so that he can minister unto them. Ministering to others was one of the hallmarks of Jesus' mortal ministry. In his great vision of that ministry, Nephi "beheld that he went forth ministering unto the people, in power and great glory" (1 Nephi 11:28). In the New Testament we find numerous examples of Jesus' ministering. He taught his disciples that unlike other leaders, he came to earth, not to be ministered to, "but to minister, and to give his life a ransom for many" (Matthew 20:28). After John's death, when Jesus went into a mountain to be alone (Greek, *kat' idian*; Matthew 14:13), he was met by a great multitude "and was moved with compassion toward them" (14:14). So he spent the day ministering to them, healing and feeding them (14:14–21). He put aside his own needs so he could minister to their needs. Likewise, he ministered to the Twelve when he washed their feet—even though, as Peter's resistance to this act reminds us, this was a duty for slaves to perform (John 13:1–10).

Unfortunately, Jesus' invitation to come unto him is often rejected, just as his invitation to come follow him was. As he stood on the Mount of Olives and overlooked Jerusalem during the last week of his mortal ministry, he lamented, "O Jerusalem, Jerusalem, thou that killest the prophets, and stonest them which are sent unto thee, how often would I have gathered thy children together, even as a hen gathereth her chickens under her wings, and ye would not!" (Matthew 23:37). As the parallel saying in 3 Nephi makes clear, Jesus sought to gather Israel in this manner in the past, he is doing so in the present and will continue to do so in the future, but at every stage his offer is rejected (3 Nephi 10:4–6). Even though he is often rejected by those who need him most, he continues to invite us to come unto him (Matthew 11:28).

Another unique aspect of this call in Matthew is that it is not extended to just a few specific individuals, as was the case when he extended the invitation of discipleship to Peter, Andrew, James, and John (Matthew 4:18–22) or the rich young man (19:16–22). In this instance his invitation is to everyone (Greek, *panta*) who labors and is heavy laden. But what does it mean to labor and be heavy laden? The Greek text suggests that the labor refers to those who are striving or struggling. In the context of the New Testament, the burdens the people are striving to carry seem to be associated with the requirements of the law of Moses. Jesus condemns the scribes and the Pharisees, in part, because "they bind heavy burdens and grievous to be borne, and lay them on men's shoulders; but they themselves will not move them with one of their fingers" (Matthew 23:4). But the text of Matthew 11:28 itself does not indicate whether the burdens are the result of external or internal forces. In other words, the text does not distinguish whether the burdens are the result of living in a mortal condition or whether they are self-imposed by sin. The text does not make a distinction because Jesus reaches out to people in both situations. Throughout his ministry Jesus reached out to the blind, the lame, the deaf, and the hungry. He cleansed the ten lepers, even though nine of them didn't stop to be grateful (Luke 17:11–19).

Jesus also ministered to those whose lives were burdened from the effects of sin. While obviously not all physical ailments are the result of sin (John 9:1–3), sometimes they are linked together (Leviticus 26:14–16; Deuteronomy 28:15, 22; Psalm 103:3). In the Book of Mormon, Zeezrom experienced a physical ailment "which was caused by the great tribulations of his mind on account of his wickedness" (Alma 15:3; see also v. 5). In the modern world, a person who abuses alcohol or the law of chastity has an increased risk of physical disease. In the New Testament example of the young man with palsy, Jesus seems to be linking his physical condition with his need for forgiveness. Jesus declared to him, "Son, be of good cheer; thy sins be forgiven thee." Immediately the scribes questioned Jesus' ability to forgive sin when they said within themselves, "This man blasphemeth. And Jesus knowing their thoughts said, Wherefore think ye evil in your hearts? For whether is easier, to say, Thy sins be forgiven thee; or to say, Arise, and walk? But that ye may know that the Son of man hath power on earth to forgive sins, (then saith he to the sick of the palsy,) Arise, take up thy bed, and go unto thine house" (Matthew 9:2–6).

Many times, however, the effect of sin is subtle. While it may not be manifested in a physical ailment, it can still be debilitating to the person entrapped in its snare. Jesus also ministers to people who are burdened in this manner. In fact, one of the major charges that the scribes and Pharisees leveled against Jesus was that he interacted with sinners and publicans. Jesus responded to these charges by teaching that such ministrations were the very heart and soul of his responsibilities. On one occasion when Jesus dined with many publicans and sinners, the Pharisees questioned his disciples, asking, "Why eateth your Master with publicans and sinners?" Jesus' response highlighted the central focus of his mission: "They that be whole need not a physician, but they that are sick" (Matthew 9:11–12). The context here shows that Jesus is referring to the spiritually sick, rather than to those with physical ailments.

On another occasion, a woman who was a sinner defied social protocol to enter a home where Jesus was eating with Simon, a Pharisee. She came and anointed Jesus' feet with her tears, wiped them dry with her hair, kissed them, and then anointed them with ointment. Simon, when he saw that Jesus accepted this act of devotion, thought to himself, "This man, if he were a prophet, would have known who and what manner of woman this is that toucheth him: for she is a sinner." Jesus, knowing his thoughts, used the opportunity to teach Simon: "And Jesus answering said unto him, Simon, I have somewhat to say unto thee. And he saith, Master, say on. There was a certain creditor which had two debtors: the one owed five hundred pence, and the other fifty. And when they had nothing to pay, he frankly forgave them both. Tell me therefore, which of them will love him most? Simon answered and said, I suppose that he, to whom he forgave most. And he said unto him, Thou hast rightly judged. And he turned to the woman, and said unto Simon, Seest thou this woman? I entered into thine house, thou gavest me no water for my feet: but she hath washed my feet with tears, and wiped them with the hairs of her head. Thou gavest me no kiss: but this woman since the time I came in hath not ceased to kiss my feet. My head with oil thou didst not anoint: but this woman hath anointed my feet with ointment. Wherefore I say unto thee, Her sins, which are many, are forgiven; for she loved much: but to whom little is forgiven, the same loveth little. And he said unto her, Thy sins are forgiven" (Luke 7:36–48).

Modern readers of Matthew 11:28 must realize that there was no time limit or expiration date on Jesus' invitation to come unto him. Certainly, we may not now be burdened with the strictures of the law of Moses; but sin is just as debilitating today as it was in the meridian of time, and there are still forces at work that can sap us of both our spiritual and physical energy even as we strive to keep the commandments, make and keep sacred covenants, and live the gospel. The righteous may still be faced with the illness and the death of loved ones. Faithful members of the Church may still be faced with financial pressures and be caught up in the devastating effects of natural disasters. Some families may have to deal with the struggles associated with a wayward child, with caring for a disabled family member, or with the sorrows they experience when their loved ones lose their lives, sometimes even when they are on the Lord's errand. These struggles and sorrows are real and cannot always be assuaged by simple platitudes. Mortals may not fully comprehend the depth of their anguish during these trials, but as Alma taught the people of Gideon, Jesus "shall go forth, suffering pains and afflictions and temptations of every kind; and this that the word might be fulfilled which saith he will take upon him the pains and the sicknesses of his people. And he will take upon him death, that he may loose the bands of death which bind his people; and he will take upon him their infirmities, that his bowels may be filled with mercy, according to the flesh, that he may know according to the flesh how to succor his people according to their infirmities" (Alma 7:11–12). Jesus' Atonement was not just for our sins; it was also for our pains, afflictions, temptations, and infirmities! The writer of Hebrews encouraged all who would read his words: "Let us therefore come boldly unto the throne of grace, that we may obtain mercy, and find grace to help in time of need" (Hebrews 4:16). The invitation, therefore, to "come unto me" is, as Elder Jeffrey R. Holland taught, "crucial. It is the key to the peace and rest we seek."[8] This is why Jesus commands us to learn of him. We need to learn of him so we can understand more deeply how his Atonement can bless our lives during these difficult experiences. We need to have personal experiences with him so that we know him from experience.

Jesus fully understood the costs he was asking of his disciples when he said, "If any man will come after me, let him deny himself, and take up his cross, and follow me" (Matthew 16:24). But he was asking no more of his disciples than he had himself paid to fulfill the will of his Father. The costs for his disciples would inevitably include trials and tribulations and sometimes the sacrifice of comforts, family, and even personal will. The last requirement may in fact be the ultimate sacrifice. Elder Neal A. Maxwell observed, "The submission of one's will is really the only uniquely personal thing we have to place on God's altar. The many other things we 'give,' brothers and sisters, are actually the things He has already given or loaned to us. However, when you and I finally submit ourselves, by letting our individual wills be swallowed up in God's will, then we are really giving something to Him! It is the only possession which is truly ours to give!"[9]

But though the costs of discipleship are assumed in Matthew 11:28–30, they are not the focal point of these verses. Rather, the emphasis is on the blessings that Jesus promises those who make the commitment to follow him and who are willing to embark upon the journey of discipleship. In these verses he identifies three specific blessings: (1) that they will have rest, (2) that Jesus' yoke is easy, and (3) that his burden is light. Although these blessings are related and often overlap, it is instructive to discuss each of them individually.

Chapter 5

REST

*J*ESUS' PROMISE OF REST MAY SEEM PARADOXICAL WITH THE notion of discipleship, especially in light of President Joseph Fielding Smith's statement that "membership in the Church is not for the idler. He who seeks an easy road to salvation must go elsewhere, it is not to be obtained in the Church."[1] Of course, President Smith knew that a leisurely stroll does not bring salvation. Jesus said it this way: "Enter ye in at the strait gate: for wide is the gate, and broad is the way, that leadeth to destruction, and many there be which go in thereat: Because strait is the gate, and narrow is the way, which leadeth unto life, and few there be that find it" (Matthew 7:13–14).

Despite Jesus' declaration about how difficult it is to find salvation, he nevertheless twice promises rest to all those who come unto him. In the first instance he promises that he will give rest:

"Come unto me, all ye that labour and are heavy laden, and I will give you rest." In the second instance, he promises that the disciples will find rest: "Take my yoke upon you, and learn of me; for I am meek and lowly in heart: and ye shall find rest unto your souls" (Matthew 11:28–30). In our discussion of these promises, we will explore two aspects of the dual promises: our responsibility to actively seek rest and three scriptural indicators that suggest when this rest will be realized.

The twice-repeated promise of rest is significant. Linguistically, it adds emphasis to the promise, and it reinforces the reality that, regardless of our personal struggles, finding rest is indeed possible. For many who feel burdened it is sometimes difficult to even imagine a time when life can be better. Therefore Jesus' double emphasis provides hope—a "perfect brightness of hope" (2 Nephi 31:20) that, as Elder Neal A. Maxwell taught, "permits us to 'press forward' even when dark clouds oppress."[2] We can be assured that it *is* possible to find rest.

In his first promise, Jesus reminds his audience that *he* is the source of this rest: "*I* will give you rest." Contrary to the myriad of advertisements that bombard our physical senses, we will not find rest in the enticements of the world, the philosophies of men, or even in clearing our busy calendars. Jesus is the great physician, the healer of our souls. And so he invites us to come unto him because he, and only he, is the source of the rest we seek. Thus Enos testifies, "For I know that in [my Redeemer] I shall rest" (Enos 1:27). But note that Jesus' promise does not necessarily guarantee an immediate reward. Although it is certainly possible to receive instantaneous relief, he does not use the present tense; rather, he uses the future tense. His promise is real, but it is important to remember that it will be realized on *his* timetable, not ours. Thus the Psalmist implores us to "rest in the Lord, and wait patiently for him" (Psalm 37:7).

In the second promise, Jesus shifts the focus from *his* steward-ship to *our* responsibility. In addition to promising that *he* will give us rest, he also promises that *we* will find rest. In this in-stance the emphasis is not on what *he* will do but on what *we* must do: "take" his yoke upon us and "learn" of him. His words invite us to become active seekers rather than passive supplicants. Thus his rest is available to all, but it is, in part, contingent upon our coming unto him. Again we may feel the weight of a paradox in his words: Can we really find rest if we are required to work to find it?

Jesus' promise of rest to us is similar to the rest he promised the Israelites. For them the promise of rest was the promise of receiving their inheritance in the promised land (Exodus 33:14). Thus, as they camped east of the Jordan River and renewed their covenant to serve the Lord, Moses taught them, "For ye are not as yet come to the rest and to the inheritance, which the Lord your God giveth you" (Deuteronomy 12:9). Here the term *rest* clearly refers to the promised land, a place where they could put down roots and not have the constant stress and effort of traveling. It took the Israelites forty years to get to the place where they were to enter into this rest—not because it took forty years to walk from Egypt to Israel but because it took forty years of wandering in the wilderness, experiencing trials and tribulations, for the Israelites to work out who they were and to demonstrate their willingness to be obedient to their God.

But Hebrews teaches that this rest was a type for a more profound rest. God's promise of rest to the Israelites was much more than a cessation of wandering in the wilderness: "Harden not your hearts, as in the provocation, in the day of temptation in the wilderness: When your fathers tempted me, proved me, and saw my works forty years. Wherefore I was grieved with that generation, and said, They do always err in their heart; and they have not known my ways. So I sware in my wrath, They shall not enter into my rest" (Hebrews 3:8–11). Although the Israelites eventually entered their promised land, according to Hebrews, they did not receive the greater rest that God sought to bestow upon his people.

What was the rest that the Israelites failed to receive? Doctrine and Covenants 84 gives us a clue. In this section we learn of the importance of the Melchizedek Priesthood, which holds "the key of the mysteries of the kingdom, even the key of the knowledge of God." This key is linked with the ordinances of the Melchizedek Priesthood: "Therefore, in the ordinances thereof, the power of godliness is manifest. And without the ordinances thereof, and the authority of the priesthood, the power of godliness is not manifest unto men in the flesh; for without this [i.e., the Melchizedek Priesthood] no man can see the face of God, even the Father, and live." It then goes on to say that Moses plainly taught these principles "to the children of Israel in the wilderness, and sought diligently to sanctify his people that they might behold the face of God; but they hardened their hearts and could not endure his presence; therefore, the Lord in his wrath, for his anger was kindled against them, swore that they should not enter into his rest while in the wilderness, which rest is the fulness of his glory" (D&C 84:19–24). Notice two things: the similarity in concepts with the discussion of rest in Hebrews (Israel hardened their hearts and did not receive their rest) and also the definition given here of rest (*"the fulness of [God's] glory"*).

That's an amazing definition and puts a whole new spin on the idea that the Sabbath is a day of rest (see below). Even though Israel entered the geographical confines of the promised land, they did not enter the spiritual realm of participating in the fulness of God's glory. Thus, they achieved a portion of the rest God wanted to give them, but not a fulness; because the Melchizedek Priesthood was taken from them, the people had to wait for a future day to have temple ordinances.

Hebrews uses this analogy with the Israelites' experience to extend a warning to the Christian Saints: "Let us therefore fear, lest, a promise being left us of entering into his rest, any of you should seem to come short of it" (Hebrews 4:1). In other words, we must make sure that as we seek to find rest we don't settle for something less than what Jesus desires to bestow upon us. Don't confuse the world's definitions of rest with that of Jesus' promise. Hebrews 4 also warns, "Let us labour therefore to enter into that rest, lest any man fall after the same example of unbelief" (4:11). Notice here the use of the word *labour*. It indicates the effort we

61

must make to enter into that rest. The Greek word from which it is translated, *spoudazō*, can mean to be especially conscientious in discharging an obligation or to be "zealous or eager, take pains, make every effort."[3] In this sense we are being told that we must be willing to pay a price to find the rest we seek. The Greek word *spoudazō*, however, also carries the connotation of the need to proceed quickly, or to hasten. So the direction to "labour" in seeking this rest also suggests an urgency to act—something that we should not procrastinate. Figuratively speaking, the message of Hebrews is that we should not let it take us 40 years to understand what *our* responsibility is in finding Jesus' rest.

The question, of course, is how we know what our responsibility is. Jesus himself gives the answer at the beginning of Matthew 11:29: "Take my yoke upon you, and learn of me." We have noted above that this command is a call to discipleship. Therefore, it is a call to take action and be counted as disciples. The scriptures give some very specific ways that we can do this. For example, Hebrews 4:3 identifies those who will enter into rest: "For we which have believed do enter into rest." The first step, then, is to believe. Professor Stephen E. Robinson's teaching has application for our discussion: This requirement to believe is not only to believe *in* Jesus but also to believe that he can do what he says he can do.[4] In this instance, we must believe that Jesus, and only Jesus, is the source of the rest that we seek, that his invitation to come unto him is genuine, and that the goal of rest is worth the price we are asked to pay. As Alma taught regarding faith, this belief may begin as just a desire, a hope; but if we will nourish it, it will grow until it gives us both the strength and will to continue the journey to our promised land (Alma 32:28–43).

Once we have developed this belief, the next step seems to be to do what Alma taught Zeezrom: "Therefore, whosoever repenteth, and hardeneth not his heart [notice this language again], he shall have claim on mercy through mine Only Begotten Son, unto a remission of his sins; and these shall enter into my rest." But, as with the Israelites, he also warns, "And whosoever will harden his heart and will do iniquity, behold, I swear in my wrath that he shall not enter into my rest" (Alma 12:34–35). Further, the Savior himself teaches, "And no unclean thing can enter into his kingdom; therefore nothing entereth into his rest save it be those who have washed their garments in my blood, because of their faith, and the repentance of all their sins, and their faithfulness unto the end" (3 Nephi 27:19). Thus we can achieve rest as we become clean. In fact, Alma taught that those of his day who had entered into "the rest of the Lord their God" (Alma 13:12) "could not look upon sin save it were with abhorrence" (Alma 13:12). Then he pleads, "And now, my brethren, I would that ye should humble yourselves before God, and bring forth fruit meet for repentance, that ye may also enter into that rest" (Alma 13:13). Our responsibility then is to repent and remain humble, understanding that we need the Atonement to help us attain rest. The Atonement enables us to *obtain* repentance as we confess our sins and participate in baptism, and it helps us to *maintain* a repentant condition. But using the

Atonement to maintain a repentant condition takes concerted effort on our part.

One important way that God has established to help us in our quest to maintain a condition of repentance is appropriately observing the Sabbath day. We've noted above that Matthew 11:28–30 is immediately followed by two Sabbath stories. It is significant that in these scriptures the concept of rest is most frequently tied to that of the Sabbath day, which, as already noted, commemorates God's determination to rest following his creative labors. In fact the Hebrew word *shabbat* means "to cease or to stop." The fourth commandment given to Moses on Mount Sinai was "Remember the sabbath day, to keep it holy. Six days shalt thou labour, and do all thy work: But the seventh day is the sabbath of the Lord thy God: in it thou shalt not do any work, thou, nor thy son, nor thy daughter, thy manservant, nor thy maidservant, nor thy cattle, nor thy stranger that is within thy gates: For in six days the Lord made heaven and earth, the sea, and all that in them is, and rested the seventh day: wherefore the Lord blessed the sabbath day, and hallowed it" (Exodus 20:8–11).

But it is also clear that the rest associated with the Sabbath day was intended by God to be much more than just a day to stop working; it was never meant to be just a passive day. As President James E. Faust taught, "Keeping the Sabbath day holy is much more than just physical rest. It involves spiritual renewal and worship."[5] Remember the Lord's definition of rest in Doctrine and Covenants 84:24: "which rest is the fulness of his glory." The Sabbath is a day of rest because we should be anxiously engaged

in activities that will help us receive a fulness of God's glory. Thus
the scriptures, while they acknowledge that it is a time to rest
from our labors, emphasize the spiritual aspect of the Sabbath day.
For example, in Exodus the Lord identifies the Sabbath as a sign
of the covenant. He declared that the Sabbath is "a sign between
me and you throughout your generations; that ye may know that
I am the Lord that doth sanctify you. . . . Wherefore the children
of Israel shall keep the sabbath, to observe the sabbath throughout their generations, for a perpetual covenant" (31:13, 16). On
the Sabbath we engage in activities that renew and reinforce our
personal and collective covenants with God. In Leviticus, the
"sabbath of rest" is equated with a holy convocation or assembly
(23:3). In the Doctrine and Covenants, the Sabbath is defined
as a "day appointed unto you to rest from your labors" (59:10),
with its purpose also being "that thou mayest more fully keep
thyself unspotted from the world" (59:9). The phrase "unspotted from the world" seems to be synonymous with "a repentant
state." Then we find specific activities that will help us achieve
this state: "Thou shalt go to the house of prayer and offer up thy
sacraments upon my holy day"; "pay thy devotions unto the Most
High"; "thou shalt offer thine oblations and thy sacraments unto
the Most High, confessing thy sins unto thy brethren, and before
the Lord" (59:9–12). Thus the Sabbath day is often called a day
of rest, not just because we cease from the labors of the world but,
more importantly, because we can participate in those activities
that will help us maintain a repentant state and prepare us to
receive a fulness of God's glory.

Having discussed the implication of Jesus' dual promise of rest and our responsibilities if we are to qualify for his rest, we are now in a position to discuss timing. When will the promise of rest be realized?

Without doubt, the ultimate rest that Jesus promises will be realized in the next life. This promise will also be partially realized in the paradise part of the spirit world, before the resurrection. Both Alma and Moroni identify a state of rest for the righteous in paradise. Alma indicates that this state is a place "where they shall rest from all their troubles and from all care, and sorrow" (Alma 40:12); Moroni looks forward to the time he will "go to rest in the paradise of God, until my spirit and body shall again reunite" (Moroni 10:34). This state of rest is in contrast to the state of the wicked who are assigned to the spirit prison. They "have no part nor portion of the Spirit of the Lord" and experience "a state of awful, fearful looking for the fiery indignation of the wrath of God upon them" (Alma 40:13–14).

But the promise of rest will be more fully realized after the Resurrection in the kingdom of God. Jesus promised nine of his Nephite disciples, "After that ye are seventy and two years old ye shall come unto me in my kingdom; and with me ye shall find rest" (3 Nephi 28:3). Lucy Mack Smith, when her two martyred sons, the Prophet Joseph and Hyrum, were brought back from Carthage, received a personal revelation. She writes, "I had for a long time braced every nerve, roused every energy of my soul and called upon God to strengthen me, but when I entered the room and saw my murdered sons extended both at once before

my eyes . . . it was too much; I sank back, crying to the Lord in
the agony of my soul, 'My God, my God, why hast thou forsaken
this family!' A voice replied, 'I have taken them to myself, that
they might have rest.'"[6]

In the book of Revelation, we find a passage that is particularly pertinent to our discussion of Matthew 11:28–30 because
it is the only other time in scripture that we have the promise
of "rest" associated with our "labour." John writes, "Here is the
patience of the saints: here are they that keep the commandments of God, and the faith of Jesus. And I heard a voice from
heaven saying unto me, Write, Blessed are the dead which die in
the Lord from henceforth: Yea, saith the Spirit, that they may rest
from their labours; and their works do follow them" (Revelation
14:12–13).

In these instances, "rest" refers to the ending of the struggles
associated with living in a mortal world—the sickness, the death
of loved ones, the persecutions, the natural disasters, the financial
struggles, and the difficulties of living with imperfect people. As
John records in Revelation, "And I saw a new heaven and a new
earth: for the first heaven and the first earth were passed away;
and there was no more sea. And I John saw the holy city, new
Jerusalem, coming down from God out of heaven, prepared as
a bride adorned for her husband. And I heard a great voice out
of heaven saying, Behold, the tabernacle of God is with men,
and he will dwell with them, and they shall be his people, and
God himself shall be with them, and be their God. And God
shall wipe away all tears from their eyes; and there shall be no

more death, neither sorrow, nor crying, neither shall there be any more pain: for the former things are passed away" (21:1–4). In this state we will find the ultimate rest that Jesus promises us. The rest we enter into in the celestial realm will also be a fulness of God's glory, where we enter into the Church of the Firstborn and become "gods, even the sons of God" (D&C 76:58; see also vv. 50–57).

Though the promise of a heavenly rest is real, it is important to remember that the promise is also available here and now while we are still in mortality. Note the teachings of Mormon: "Wherefore, I would speak unto you that are of the church, that are the peaceable followers of Christ, and that have obtained a sufficient hope by which ye can enter into the rest of the Lord, from this time henceforth until ye shall rest with him in heaven" (Moroni 7:3). Mormon speaks to the members of the Church, the peaceable followers of Christ, who have already obtained a hope that they can enter into rest. Note the language: "Ye can enter into the rest of the Lord, *from this time*" (emphasis added). The promise of this rest was available to them during Mormon's ministry and would continue to be available until they experienced the heavenly rest. Remember that the Lord's promise to Israel of rest or the fulness of God's glory, even though they rejected it, was available to them in mortality at Mount Sinai (D&C 84:23–24). Mormon's teachings remind us that if we think of Jesus' promise in Matthew only in terms of a heavenly reward, we might fail to recognize the myriad of ways that he seeks to bless us here and now.

What are some of the ways that Jesus will bless us with rest in mortality? President Joseph F. Smith identifies one way that we can find rest from spiritual turmoil: "The ancient prophets speak of 'entering into God's rest'; what does it mean? To my mind, it means entering into the knowledge and love of God, having faith in his purpose and in his plan, to such an extent that we know we are right, and that we are not hunting for something else, we are not disturbed by every wind of doctrine, or by the cunning and craftiness of men who lie in wait to deceive. We know of the doctrine that it is of God, and we do not ask any questions of anybody about it; they are welcome to their opinions, to their ideas and to their vagaries. The man who has reached that degree of faith in God that all doubt and fear have been cast from him, he has entered into 'God's rest,' and he need not fear the vagaries of men, nor their cunning craftiness, by which they seek to deceive and mislead him from the truth. I pray that we may all enter into God's rest—rest from doubt, from fear, from apprehension of danger, rest from religious turmoil of the world."[7] At another time, commenting specifically on Moroni 7:3, he taught, "This is a very significant passage. The rest here referred to is not physical rest, for there is no such thing as physical rest in the Church of Jesus Christ. Reference is made to the spiritual rest and peace which are born from a settled conviction of the truth in the minds of men. We may thus enter into the rest of the Lord today, by coming to an understanding of the truths of the gospel. No people is more entitled to this rest—this peace of the spirit—than are the members of the Church."[8] In other words, disciples of Jesus Christ may not know the answers to all questions, but that does not cause us to become absorbed in an intellectual frenzy, in which searching for the answer to the unknown may become our focus to the exclusion of the many glorious truths that we do know. Rather, we are at peace with our testimony of the gospel and understand that it is all right to set aside some unanswered questions for a time because we understand that eventually all things will be revealed and understood. In this situation, we are reminded of Jesus' teachings in Matthew immediately before his invitation, "Come unto me, all ye that labour and are heavy laden." The Lord teaches us that the most important thing, a knowledge of the Father and the Son, which gives us the lens of clarity for so many of our questions, can only be known through revelation (Matthew 11:27).

Personal revelation can bring us the rest we seek from a myriad of travails. We feel the pain and pathos of the Prophet Joseph's cries while in Liberty Jail. In many ways, his cries represent our own cries of anguish as we seek peace and rest, the cries of pain from a parent who has lost a child, the anguish of someone debilitated by a progressive or incurable disease, or the frustration of someone weighed down with the burdens of unrelenting responsibility. The Prophet wrote:

"O God, where art thou? And where is the pavilion that covereth thy hiding place?

"How long shall thy hand be stayed, and thine eye, yea thy pure eye, behold from the eternal heavens the wrongs of thy people and of thy servants, and thine ear be penetrated with their cries?

"Yea, O Lord, how long shall they suffer these wrongs and unlawful oppressions, before thine heart shall be softened toward them, and thy bowels be moved with compassion toward them?

"O Lord God Almighty, maker of heaven, earth, and seas, and of all things that in them are, and who controllest and subjectest the devil, and the dark and benighted dominion of Sheol— stretch forth thy hand; let thine eye pierce; let thy pavilion be taken up; let thy hiding place no longer be covered; let thine ear be inclined; let thine heart be softened, and thy bowels moved with compassion toward us.

"Let thine anger be kindled against our enemies; and, in the fury of thine heart, with thy sword avenge us of our wrongs.

"Remember thy suffering saints, O our God; and thy servants will rejoice in thy name forever" (D&C 121:1–6).

The revelation the Lord gives to the Prophet in response is the same he gives to us in our darkest times:

"My son, peace be unto thy soul; thine adversity and thine afflictions shall be but a small moment;

"And then, if thou endure it well, God shall exalt thee on high; thou shalt triumph over all thy foes" (D&C 121:7–8).

Though Jesus' promise does not remove the pain and suffering, it will enable us to find the rest we seek in him. The promise of rest also incorporates two additional promises—that the yoke will be easy and the burdens will be made light.

71

V

Chapter 6

AN EASY YOKE

$\mathscr{P}$EOPLE LIVING IN THE FIRST CENTURY AFTER CHRIST WERE
more familiar with yokes and their use than we are today.
Originally, the word *yoke* described a simple instrument that
bound draft animals, usually two oxen, together at the neck to
help them work together. Later, a modified device was placed
around the necks of prisoners to control and discipline them.
Similarly, a wooden frame was fitted to a person's shoulders to
assist him or her in carrying a heavy load of two equal portions—
one on the right side and the other on the left side. Each of these
devices was known as a yoke.

Over time, *yoke* took on a figurative nuance and was widely
used as an important metaphor in the ancient Near East, including in the Old Testament. It was always used as a symbol of "control, ownership, or service."[1] For example, in Genesis, Isaac tells

Esau that some day he will be free from Jacob's control: "Behold, thy dwelling shall be the fatness of the earth, and of the dew of heaven from above; and by thy sword shalt thou live, and shalt serve thy brother [Jacob]; and it shall come to pass when thou shalt have the dominion, that thou shalt *break his yoke from off thy neck*" (Genesis 27:39–40; emphasis added; see also Jeremiah 5:5). Later, the Lord warned Israel that if they broke the covenant they would "serve thine enemies which the Lord shall send against thee, in hunger, and in thirst, and in nakedness, and in want of all things: and he shall *put a yoke of iron upon thy neck*, until he have destroyed thee" (Deuteronomy 28:48; emphasis added). "Yoke" is also used in the Bible to symbolize a variety of evils—including burdensome taxes, oppression, and slavery (1 Kings 12:11).

Increasingly over time in Judaism, it was common to talk about God's placing upon Israel the "yoke" of the Law—demonstrating lordship over his covenant people. They could either bear the yoke of the Torah through covenant loyalty, through obedience, or they could cast off the yoke and choose to wear the yoke of false gods. Realistically, it was impossible to wear two yokes at the same time and therefore one had to choose who to obey. In the first century, Rabbi Nehunya ben Ha-Kanah said, "He that takes upon himself the yoke of the Law, from him shall be taken away the yoke of the kingdom and the yoke of worldly care; but he that throws off the yoke of the Law, upon him shall be laid the yoke of the kingdom and the yoke of worldly care."[2]

Jesus, just as his contemporaries, also used the yoke as a metaphor when he offered "my yoke" to those who would come unto him. However, as was the case here, Jesus often provides surprising, even counterintuitive insights and teachings. Later, the cross must have also become part of the allusion since the term for yoke (*zygos*) was the same term used to describe the cross beam Jesus carried to Golgotha.[3] Therefore, Jesus talked about taking upon us not only a yoke but a cross: "And he that taketh not his cross, and followeth after me, is not worthy of me" (Matthew 10:38).

Figuratively, Jesus knew that every person wears a yoke—no one is free from an obligation, duty, or loyalty to someone or something. In our modern individualistic society, we may falsely assume that we are completely independent individuals with no masters. However, this is not true. In choosing to reject Jesus' invitation to take upon ourselves his easy yoke, we invariably find ourselves wearing a harsher one. Elder D. Todd Christofferson emphasized this point when he quoted Catholic bishop Fulton J. Sheen's famous observation, "We would not accept the yoke of Christ; so now we must tremble at the yoke of Caesar."[4]

The reality is that any of us can become slaves to worshiping ourselves, fashion, passions, power, money, popularity, political parties, sports teams, or some other cause that has captured our hearts and minds. In the end we are forced to choose one above all else (Joshua 24:15). In this regard, Jesus taught, "No man can serve two masters: for either he will hate the one, and love the other; or else he will hold to the one, and despise the other. Ye cannot serve God and mammon" (Matthew 6:24).

In offering us his yoke, Jesus said of it, "For my yoke is easy, and my burden is light" (Matthew 11:30). The paradox is obvious—the yoke is usually a sign of humiliation or dominance, demonstrated by the fact that the enemy places his foot on the neck of the captured person while placing the yoke around the prisoner's neck, whereas Jesus indicates that his yoke will bring rest and comfort to those who are willing to wear it. Demonstrating the difference between Jesus and other taskmasters, no one is forced to take his yoke, just as no one is forced to come unto him in the first place. Elder Bruce C. Hafen reminds us, "As an act of will, we must take the first step that begins the journey."[5]

Interestingly, the yoke Jesus gives us is easy because what he requires of us is rather simple—focus on the essentials of loving God and your neighbor (Matthew 22:36–40). Paradoxically, it is at the same time more challenging because it also requires us to love our enemies (5:44). For Jesus said, "That except your righteousness shall exceed the righteousness of the scribes and Pharisees, ye shall in no case enter into the kingdom of heaven" (5:20). In this sense, we could say that Jesus' yoke is at once more demanding while at the same time more rewarding.

Elder Neal A. Maxwell said, "Consecration, likewise, is not shoulder-shrugging acceptance, but, instead, shoulder-squaring to better bear the yoke,"[6] suggesting that to bear the yoke of Christ requires more than simply being busy at church. Elder Maxwell noted, "It would change the entire Church if in every ward, we could have just three or four more families who became truly consecrated disciples of Jesus Christ instead of just being active in the Church."[7] Elder Hafen adds, "We talk often about the distinction between being active in the Church and being inactive. We should perhaps also talk more about the additional difference between being active and being a truly consecrated disciple."[8]

Unlike kings, slave owners, and others who exercise authority over us, Jesus is a gentle master who has no agenda except to heal and save all those who come unto him. To emphasize this insight, Matthew quotes the longest scripture passage from the Old Testament cited in his Gospel, shortly after recording Jesus' invitation and promise. It is a beautiful text known as the "Servant Prophecy" from Isaiah 42, where Isaiah portrays the Messiah as a tender, kind, and humble servant of God who would not even break a bruised reed or quench a smoldering wick: "Behold my servant [Greek, *pais*, 'son or servant'], whom I have chosen; my beloved, in whom my soul is well pleased: I will put my spirit upon him, and he shall shew judgment to the Gentiles. He shall not strive, nor cry [He will not wrangle or cry aloud]; neither shall any man hear his voice in the streets. A bruised reed shall he not break, and smoking flax shall he not quench, till he send forth judgment unto victory. And in his name shall the Gentiles trust" (Matthew 12:18–21). Instead of a Messianic warrior, God's Son is compassionate—a loving king who takes care of us. One New Testament scholar adds, "More to the point, he will be gentle on the weak, the weary, the tenderhearted, the bruised and abused, the downtrodden."[9]

We may wonder how Jesus' yoke can be easy. How does choosing to wear it daily become a blessing to us? Like a polished diamond, the metaphor is multi-faceted. Latter-day prophets and apostles have provided inspired answers to these questions, offering insights that will allow us to consider Jesus' yoke in new ways. For example, Elder Maxwell observed, "[Christ's] yoke, when fully and squarely placed upon us, is much lighter than the weight of sin. No burden is as heavy as the burden of the 'natural man'! The annoying load of ambivalence and the hecticness of hesitation produce their own aggravations and frustrations."[10]

Elsewhere Elder Maxwell wrote: "Happily, the commandment [to take his yoke upon us] carries an accompanying and compensating promise: 'and ye shall find rest unto your souls.' (Matthew 11:29.) This special form of rest surely includes the shedding of certain needless burdens, such as fatiguing insincerity, exhausting hypocrisy, and the strength-sapping quest for praise and power.

"Those of us who fail in one way or another almost always do so because we carry unnecessary and heavy baggage. Thus overloaded, we then feel sorry for ourselves."[11]

President Thomas S. Monson indicated that through obeying God's gentle commands we take upon ourselves the yoke Jesus offers us—just as Jesus took the yoke given him: "What personal bridges did He build and cross here in mortality, showing us the way to follow? He knew mortality would be filled with dangers and difficulties. He declared: 'Come unto me, all ye that labour and are heavy laden, and I will give you rest. Take my yoke upon you, and learn of me; for I am meek and lowly in heart: and ye shall find rest unto your souls. For my yoke is easy, and my burden is light.' Jesus provided the bridge of obedience. He was an unfailing example of personal obedience as He kept the commandments of His Father."[12]

Elder Jeffrey R. Holland highlighted the remedy that heals us: "I speak to those who are facing personal trials and family struggles, those who endure conflicts fought in the lonely foxholes of the heart, those trying to hold back floodwaters of despair that sometimes wash over us like a tsunami of the soul. I wish to speak particularly to you who feel your lives are broken, seemingly beyond repair. To all such I offer the surest and sweetest remedy that I know. It is found in the clarion call the Savior of the world Himself gave. He said it in the beginning of His ministry, and He said it in the end. He said it to believers, and He said it to those who were not so sure. He said to everyone, whatever their personal problems might be: 'Come unto me, all ye that labour and are heavy laden, and I will give you rest. Take my yoke upon you, and learn of me; for I am meek and lowly in heart: and ye shall find rest unto your souls' (Matthew 11:28–29)."[13]

Another reason for taking Jesus' yoke upon us is to learn to be like him. Elder Maxwell noted: "Real adoration of Jesus as our Savior but also as the perfect leader will lead us to emulation of Him. After all, He said, 'Take my yoke upon you, and learn of me; for I am meek and lowly' [Matthew 11:29]. Brothers and sisters, we cannot really learn any deep or lasting things about Jesus unless we take His yoke upon us. Then, though on our small scales compared to His, the relevant experiences will teach us keenly and deeply about Him and His divine attributes. There is nothing abstract about it at all. It becomes a very personal thing for us."[14]

Jesus also indicates that we, as disciples, become lifelong learners. In this regard Elder Maxwell has observed, "Unlike servitude to sin, by wearing his yoke we truly learn of the Yoke Master in what is an education for eternity as well as for mortality."[15]

Finally, Elder M. Russell Ballard testified that we obtain rest only through the efficacy of Jesus' Atonement: "Beyond that we need to remember that Christ came to remove guilt by forgiving those who repent (Alma 24:10). He came to bring peace to the troubled soul. 'Peace I leave with you,' He said. 'My peace I give unto you: not as the world giveth, give I unto you. Let not your heart be troubled, neither let it be afraid' (John 14:27). Through the miraculous Atonement He urges us to 'take my yoke upon you, . . . and ye shall find rest unto your souls' (Matthew 11:29)."[16]

Matthew describes the early days of Jesus' mortal ministry when he "went about all Galilee, teaching in their synagogues, and preaching the gospel of the kingdom, and healing all manner of sickness and all manner of disease among the people" (4:23). Inviting those who would listen to come unto him, Jesus said that they should take his yoke upon them and learn of him. Paradoxically, in so doing Jesus gives us an easy yoke, creating a light burden because he bears it with us. In this, Jesus turned the world upside down.

Chapter 7

A LIGHT BURDEN

IN THE FINAL PROMISE THAT JESUS MAKES TO THOSE WHO come unto him, we are again confronted with a paradox: "My burden is light" (Matthew 11:30). How can a burden be light? The Greek word for "burden" is *fortion*, used in only four other places in the New Testament: Matthew 23:4; Luke 11:46; Acts 27:10; Galatians 6:5. In each of these passages the word refers to things that are heavy to bear: the burdens of Pharisaical requirements that are "grievous to be borne" (Matthew 23:4; Luke 11:46), the cargo in a ship (Acts 27:10), and the personal burdens borne by those who follow Christ (Galatians 6:5). But how can something that is heavy be light? This, again, is a paradox. As one scholar notes, "Perhaps we are intended to sense the paradox in being told by a man who makes such stringent demands on his disciples that the burden he imposes is light! The paradox is to be resolved in the experience of the Christian life."[1] In other words, the paradox can only be resolved for the disciple as he or she puts Jesus' promise to the test.

Before we discuss some specific burdens that Jesus promises to make light, it is important to understand a principle taught in the Book of Mormon that will help us recognize *when* Jesus lightens our burdens. We find this principle in the book of Mosiah, where two groups of Nephites living in the land of Nephi find themselves trying to flourish under great burdens. One group, under the direction of Alma the Elder, sought freedom from the spiritual oppression of the wicked king Noah. They fled into the wilderness and eventually settled in the land of Helam. Though they enjoyed their freedom for a time, eventually the priests of Noah found them and, with the authority and help of the Lamanites, placed them in bondage: "And now it came to pass that Amulon began to exercise authority over Alma and his brethren, and began to persecute him, and cause that his children should persecute their children . . . and put tasks upon them, and put taskmasters over them" (Mosiah 24:8–9). The other group, under the direction of King Limhi and Gideon, were also burdened by the Lamanites' oppression. They forced Limhi's people to pay taxes of "one half of all they possessed" (19:26), and the Lamanites "would smite them on their cheeks, and exercise authority over them; and began to put heavy burdens upon their backs, and drive them as they would a dumb ass" (21:3). In response to these burdens, both these persecuted groups cried mightily to the Lord for deliverance (21:14; 24:10–13). What is important to recognize in these two stories is that though the Lord responded to their prayers of supplication, he did so in very different ways.

In the case of King Limhi's group, the Lord softened the hearts of the Lamanites so they eased the burdens of Limhi's group, although he did not at that time deliver them out of bondage (21:15). In contrast, the Lord promised Alma's group that he would "ease the burdens which are put upon your shoulders, that even you cannot feel them upon your backs, even while you are in bondage." As a result, "the burdens which were laid upon Alma and his brethren were made light; yea, the Lord did strengthen them that they could bear up their burdens with ease, and they did submit cheerfully and with patience to all the will of the Lord" (24:14–15). While the Lord lightened the burdens of Limhi's group by removing some of the burdens, he did not remove any of the burdens for Alma's group. Instead he lightened them by making the people stronger. This was a very different response from his dealings with Limhi's group.

It is probably fair to say that most people, when they pray for the Lord's help to lighten their burdens, hope that he will respond in the same way he did with King Limhi's group: remove some of the burdens. We would like him to remove the burdens of financial stress, physical illness or limitations, a guilty conscience, or the cravings of an addiction. Sometimes he does answer our cries for deliverance in this manner, but the story of Alma's group shows that he does not always respond in this way. The reality is that many times the Lord makes our burdens lighter not by removing them but by strengthening us so that we are better able to bear them. For example, he may not always send us an unexpected check in the mail when we are burdened with financial stress, but he may help us to develop a simpler lifestyle or put people in our path who can help us find ways to make ends meet with the money we have available to us. These two examples offer a caution: If we are not careful, we may fail to recognize the hand of God in our lives because we have preconceived expectations about how he should lighten our burdens. Part of being a disciple and coming unto Christ is a willingness to allow our will to be swallowed up in his will, just as Christ has allowed his will to be swallowed up in the will of the Father (Mosiah 15:7). It is a mark of spiritual maturity to be able to recognize that as mortals we have a limited view of eternity and an imperfect understanding of what will be eternally beneficial for us. We are blessed when we are able to recognize the complete tapestry of ways that the hand of God is manifest in our lives.

Recognizing this important principle about how Christ can lighten our burdens, we can now discuss the question, "What are the burdens that Jesus promises to make light?" In some ways this is a difficult question to answer because in Matthew 11 Jesus does not elaborate on what he means. On the one hand, in the text the burdens are parallel with the yoke mentioned at the beginning of the verse. So the immediate context suggests that the burdens refer to the Pharisaical interpretation of the law of Moses that, as Jesus says, is grievous to be borne. Though that was an important point for the original readers of Matthew's Gospel, for modern readers this interpretation has little application in our daily lives. In the broader context of Matthew, however, the burdens seem to refer to the costs of discipleship. With this interpretation we believe that modern readers can find a wealth of application.

What are some of the costs of discipleship that can feel burdensome? The scriptures are replete with examples. Here we will discuss just three: the burden we may feel in accepting and fulfilling Church callings; the burden we will experience from living in a mortal world; and the burden with which we struggle on account of personal sin.

First, there are times when a call to serve in the kingdom of God may feel like a burden that is too heavy to bear. We may feel inadequate to fulfill the responsibilities of the calling, or it may be that those responsibilities will take us out of our comfort zone. Certainly, this is how Enoch and Moses felt when they received their prophetic calls. Enoch's response was, "Why is it that I have found favor in thy sight, and am but a lad, and all the people hate me; for I am slow of speech; wherefore am I thy servant?" (Moses 6:31). Moses' response to his call was simply, "Who am I, that I should go unto Pharaoh, and that I should bring forth the children of Israel out of Egypt?" (Exodus 3:11). Some of us may even feel as Jonah did, who tried to escape the burden of the prophetic call and sought to flee from the responsibility (Jonah 1:3).

Of course the feeling of inadequacy is not limited to prophetic callings. The burden may also feel overwhelming, for example, for people who are called to play the piano in Primary when they have limited piano skills, or if they are called to teach

Gospel Doctrine when they do not view themselves as gospel scholars. Only rarely does it seem that the Lord calls people to serve in callings where there is no need for growth and humble reliance upon the Lord. Rather, the very nature of callings in the Church, whether the call is to be the prophet or a nursery leader, is that the individual will grow in both their talents and their spiritual capacity. If an individual does not feel a sense of inad- equacy on some level then there will be no sense of dependence upon the Lord.

The Lord responded to Enoch's protest by declaring, "Go forth and do as I have commanded thee, and no man shall pierce thee. Open thy mouth, and it shall be filled, and I will give thee utterance, for all flesh is in my hands, and I will do as seemeth me good" (Moses 6:32). In this case the Lord promised to make Enoch's burden light by protecting him from his enemies' attacks and by healing his speech impediment. In Moses' case, the Lord promised that he would be with Moses and gave him certain in- formation as an evidence of that gift (Exodus 3:12–14). Of course the promise to lighten these burdens did not mean that either Enoch or Moses would be carefree for the rest of their prophetic ministry. Jesus' promise in Matthew 11:30 is not that he will re- move the burdens—only that he will make them bearable. Both Enoch and Moses continued to face challenges, but after these initial experiences they were able to move forward with confi- dence that the Lord would continue to make them equal to each new burden as it confronted them.

Likewise, the Lord promises that he will lighten the burdens that accompany modern callings in the Church. President Thomas S. Monson teaches: "Some of you may be shy by nature or consider yourselves inadequate to respond affirmatively to a calling. Remember that this work is not yours and mine alone. It is the Lord's work, and when we are on the Lord's errand, we are entitled to the Lord's help. Remember that whom the Lord calls, the Lord qualifies."[2] In other words, just as he did for Alma and his people, Christ helps us become equal to the task. He helps us to develop the skills that we need. He will help the shy person find the courage to stand up in front of a class and teach or give a talk or knock on someone's door. He will help magnify an individual's talents and skills as he or she continues to work to develop them. He will help missionaries, young or older, learn languages and endure the rigors of missionary service. These transformations are sometimes immediate, as they seem to have been when Paul was baptized. "And straightway he preached Christ in the synagogues, that he is the Son of God. But all that heard him were amazed, and said; Is not this he that destroyed them which called on this name in Jerusalem, and came hither for that intent, that he might bring them bound unto the chief priests? But Saul increased the more in strength, and confounded the Jews which dwelt at Damascus, proving that this is very Christ" (Acts 9:20–22). More often, however, the transformation proceeds over a period of time. Sometimes we may not recognize the hand of the Lord until we are looking back in hindsight. Nevertheless, the scriptures give us confidence that the Lord will indeed make our burdens light as we have the faith to accept his call. Elder

Neal A. Maxwell taught, "God does not begin by asking us about our ability, but only about our availability, and if we then prove our dependability, he will increase our capability."[3]

A second kind of burden that disciples often experience is the effects of sickness, pain, and death, all of which are an integral part of living in a telestial world. As a consequence of the Fall, God told Eve, "I will greatly multiply thy sorrow and thy conception. In sorrow thou shalt bring forth children, and thy desire shall be to thy husband, and he shall rule over thee." Likewise, to Adam he said, "Cursed shall be the ground for thy sake; in sorrow shalt thou eat of it all the days of thy life. Thorns also, and thistles shall it bring forth to thee, and thou shalt eat the herb of the field. By the sweat of thy face shalt thou eat bread, until thou shalt return unto the ground—for thou shalt surely die—for out of it wast thou taken: for dust thou wast, and unto dust shalt thou return" (Moses 4:22–25). Life in mortality was meant to be hard. There is no way we can get around that fact. As the Lord told Abraham, mortality is a time to "prove them herewith, to see if they will do all things whatsoever the Lord their God shall command them" (Abraham 3:25).

Nevertheless, when Adam and Eve learned about the mission of Jesus Christ and received the Holy Ghost, they recognized the great blessing these trials would be for them: "And in that day Adam blessed God and was filled, and began to prophesy concerning all the families of the earth, saying: Blessed be the name of God, for because of my transgression my eyes are opened, and in this life I shall have joy, and again in the flesh I shall see

God. And Eve, his wife, heard all these things and was glad, saying: Were it not for our transgression we never should have had seed, and never should have known good and evil, and the joy of our redemption, and the eternal life which God giveth unto all the obedient. And Adam and Eve blessed the name of God" (Moses 5:10–12). They understood the blessings that come from the struggle in mortality, "and they made all things known unto their sons and their daughters" (5:12).

Even with this knowledge, the paradox between the struggle and the blessing has continued to vex Adam and Eve's posterity. This is the very principle that is the focus of the book of Job. As the book opens, Job is described as a righteous man, one who "was perfect and upright, and one that feared God, and eschewed evil" (1:1). As such he prospered in both his family and his wealth. In the narrative that follows Satan argues that the only reason Job is so righteous is because the Lord has protected him from the natural consequences of mortality—hardship, disappointment, pain, and suffering—and has instead "made an hedge about him, and about his house, and about all that he hath on every side" (1:10). If, Satan argues, the Lord were to "put forth thine hand now, and touch all that he hath . . . he will curse thee to thy face" (1:11). We then learn that in one day Job lost all of his children and all of his flocks. As devastating as this was, Job recognized the transient nature of mortality: "Naked came I out of my mother's womb, and naked shall I return thither: the Lord gave, and the Lord hath taken away; blessed be the name of the Lord" (1:21). But that was not the end of his suffering. On another day Job is struck down with "sore boils from the sole of his foot unto his crown" (2:7). It is hard to imagine anything more uncomfortable. If Job stood, the boils on his feet would cause great pain, and if he sat down or lay down he would experience more of the same. It would also mean that he would not be able to find a comfortable position to go to sleep. Over time the lack of sleep would have only exacerbated the situation. But, although the book of Job mentions the familial and physical struggles, the emphasis is on Job's spiritual burden as he struggled to receive answers from God to understand why all these trials had suddenly descended upon him. When answers didn't come immediately, those burdens were magnified by a loss of hope that his life would ever improve. "My days are swifter than a weaver's shuttle, and are spent without hope" (7:6).

Job's experiences with the death of loved ones and severe physical challenges, although exceptional in their extremity, are typical of challenges that all humans experience in some form during mortality. Likewise, the reaction of Job's wife and friends to his predicament reflect some of the human reactions to adversity in every age. No doubt devastated by her husband's afflictions, Job's wife encourages him to "curse God, and die," but he responds, "What? shall we receive good at the hand of God, and shall we not receive evil?" (2:9–10). Job's friends, Eliphaz, Bildad, and Zophar, each in his own way, tell Job that these kinds of trials must be the result of his personal sin (4:7–9; 8:1–6, 20; 11:6, 14–15). Their responses to Job's difficulties are certainly not unique to them. Sin does bring unwelcome consequences. But it does not follow, as Jesus taught his disciples, that all suffering is the result of sin (John 9:1–3). Speaking of suffering, Elder Richard G. Scott has taught: "No one wants adversity. Trials, disappointments, sadness, and heartache come to us from two basically different sources. Those who transgress the laws of God will always have those challenges. The other reason for adversity is to accomplish the Lord's own purposes in our life that we may receive the refinement that comes from testing." Then Elder Scott continues, *"It is vitally important for each of us to identify from which of these two sources come our trials and challenges, for the corrective action is very different"* (emphasis added).[4] Job's friends confused these two sources, and their focus on how Job must have sinned needlessly postponed the relief for which he yearned.

Although the Lord eventually restored to Job twice as much as he had lost (Job 42:10–17), this recompense was not what lightened Job's burden. Rather, the lightening came when God personally responded to Job's heavenward cries. Even so, God's response was probably not what Job was expecting. He does not give a reason for the suffering; instead God reminds Job of his omnipotence, particularly in comparison to humanity's limitations. God's response is a reminder that he is in control. We are reminded of Isaiah's teaching: "For my thoughts are not your thoughts, neither are your ways my ways, saith the Lord. For as the heavens are higher than the earth, so are my ways higher than your ways, and my thoughts than your thoughts" (Isaiah 55:8–9). Job's humble response to his revelation is instructive: "I know that thou canst do every thing, and that no thought can be withholden from thee. Who is he that hideth counsel without knowledge? therefore have I uttered that I understood not; things too wonderful for me, which I knew not. Hear, I beseech thee, and I will speak: I will demand of thee, and declare thou unto me. I have heard of thee by the hearing of the ear: but now mine eye seeth thee" (Job 42:2–5). The lightening of Job's burden came as the Lord communed with him. Job once thought that he understood the power of God, but now he realized just how limited was his understanding of God. Through this revelation Job began to see with greater clarity the power and purposes of God. Job's burden was lightened not because God removed his burdens but because he came to know God's will. Only then did the physical blessings come.

The burdens of mortality that disciples face today can be symbolized by Job's experiences. They may not be exactly the same, but they often feel just as debilitating. In such cases, the message of Job is just as pertinent today as it was in antiquity. As paradoxical as it seems, burdens can be lightened through achieving an understanding of the Lord and his purposes. Elder Jeffrey R. Holland thus assured us: "As you labor to know [God], and to know that he knows you; as you invest your time—and inconvenience—in quiet, unassuming service, you will indeed find that 'his angels [have] charge concerning thee: and in their hands they shall bear thee up.' [Matthew 4:6.] It may not come quickly. It probably won't come quickly, but there is purpose in the time it takes. Cherish your spiritual burdens because God will converse with you through them."[5]

It is in these very personal moments of communion that we can feel the lightening of both our physical and spiritual burdens. President Gordon B. Hinckley recounts an example of "a friend who had escaped from his native land. With the fall of his nation, he was arrested and interned. His wife and children were able to get away, but for three years and more he was a prisoner without means of communication with those he loved. The food was wretched, the living conditions oppressive, with no prospects for improvement. 'What sustained you through all those dark days?' I asked. He responded: 'My faith; my faith in the Lord Jesus Christ. I put my burdens on him, and then they seemed so much the lighter.'"[6]

A third kind of burden comes through personal sin. All mortals, to a greater or lesser extent, carry this burden. Paul taught the Romans, "For all have sinned, and come short of the glory of God" (Romans 3:23), and the apostle John declared, "If we say that we have no sin, we deceive ourselves, and the truth is not in us" (1 John 1:8). Perhaps the greatest scriptural example of how Jesus lightens the burden of sin is that of Alma the Younger. In his account, Alma described in some detail both the physical, spiritual, and emotional burden of sin as well as the lifting of that burden when he finally recognized his need to come unto Christ. In his vivid description of the burden of his sins, Alma told his son Helaman: "I was racked with eternal torment, for my soul was harrowed up to the greatest degree and racked with all my sins.

"Yea, I did remember all my sins and iniquities, for which I was tormented with the pains of hell; yea, I saw that I had rebelled against my God, and that I had not kept his holy commandments.

"Yea, and I had murdered many of his children, or rather led them away unto destruction; yea, and in fine so great had been my iniquities, that the very thought of coming into the presence of my God did rack my soul with inexpressible horror.

"Oh, thought I, that I could be banished and become extinct both soul and body, that I might not be brought to stand in the presence of my God, to be judged of my deeds" (Alma 36:12–15).

As serious as these sins were (Alma likened them to spiritual murder), the real emphasis of the account is the power of Jesus Christ to remove the burden of his guilt:

"And it came to pass that as I was thus racked with torment, while I was harrowed up by the memory of my many sins, behold, I remembered also to have heard my father prophesy unto the people concerning the coming of one Jesus Christ, a Son of God, to atone for the sins of the world.

"Now, as my mind caught hold upon this thought, I cried within my heart: O Jesus, thou Son of God, have mercy on me, who am in the gall of bitterness, and am encircled about by the everlasting chains of death.

"And now, behold, when I thought this, I could remember my pains no more; yea, I was harrowed up by the memory of my sins no more.

"And oh, what joy, and what marvelous light I did behold; yea, my soul was filled with joy as exceeding as was my pain" (Alma 36:17–20).

Not only did the Atonement lighten Alma's burden of guilt but it transformed him from a being who once despaired at the idea of coming into God's presence (Alma 36:15) into one who longed to be with God (v. 22). Alma's experience is proof of what the author of Hebrews hoped for all Christians: "Let us therefore come boldly unto the throne of grace, that we may obtain mercy, and find grace to help in time of need" (Hebrews 4:16).

This power is real, and it is just as real today as it was in Alma's day. Elder Dallin H. Oaks describes two powerful experiences of persons who were burdened with their own sin or with the sin of a loved one. In both of these instances the individuals' burdens were lightened as they turned to the Savior for help: "A man wrote a General Authority about how the power of the Atonement helped him with his problem of same-gender attraction. He had been excommunicated for serious transgression that violated his temple covenants and his responsibilities to his children. He had to choose whether to attempt to live the gospel or whether to continue a course contrary to its teachings. 'I knew it would be difficult,' he wrote, 'but I didn't realize what I would have to go through.' His letter describes the emptiness and loneliness and the incredible pain he experienced from deep within his soul as he sought to return. He prayed mightily for forgiveness, sometimes for hours at a time. He was sustained by reading the scriptures, by the companionship of a loving bishop, and by priesthood blessings. But what finally made the difference was the help of the Savior. He explained: 'It [was] only through Him and His Atonement. . . . I now feel an overwhelming gratitude. My

HE WILL GIVE YOU REST

pains have been almost more than I could bear at times, and yet they were so small compared to what He suffered. Where there once was darkness in my life, there is now love and gratitude.'"[7]

In the second instance the burden came because of the sin of a loved one. These burdens are also very real. "A woman whose marriage was threatened by her husband's addiction to pornography wrote how she stood beside him for five pain-filled years until, as she said, 'through the gift of our precious Savior's glorious Atonement and what He taught me about forgiveness, [my husband] finally is free—and so am I.' As one who needed no cleansing from sin but sought a loved one's deliverance from captivity, she wrote this advice: 'Commune with the Lord. . . . He is your best friend! He knows your pain because He has felt it for you already. He is ready to carry that burden. Trust Him enough to place it at His feet and allow Him to carry it for you. Then you can have your anguish replaced with His peace, in the very depths of your soul.'"[8]

It is important that modern disciples do not get caught up in a sense of false security, thinking that because they have committed no major sin, they have no need for the Atonement. Remember Paul's teaching: "All have sinned" (Romans 3:23). All of us need the redemptive power of the Atonement in our lives. Even the righteous can be burdened with sin. We find an example of this situation in Nephi's psalm. When Lehi died and Nephi realized that the prophetic mantle was now his, he keenly felt the burden of his sin and wrote: "Notwithstanding the great goodness of the Lord, in showing me his great and marvelous works, my heart exclaimeth: O wretched man that I am! Yea, my heart sorroweth because of my flesh; my soul grieveth because of mine iniquities. I am encompassed about, because of the temptations and the sins which do so easily beset me. . . . Why should my heart weep and my soul linger in the valley of sorrow, and my flesh waste away, and my strength slacken, because of mine afflictions? And why should I yield to sin, because of my flesh? Yea, why should I give way to temptations, that the evil one have place in my heart to destroy my peace and afflict my soul?" (2 Nephi 4:17–18, 26–27). In some ways it is hard to even imagine what sins Nephi could have committed that would cause him to lament in this way. After all, Nephi was the good son, unlike his brothers Laman and Lemuel. Speaking of Nephi's lament, Elder Maxwell has taught, "The prophet Nephi, who had progressed and advanced spiritually to a remarkable degree, still lamented about 'sins which do so easily beset me' (2 Nephi 4:18). Obviously, Nephi's sins were not major. But just as God cannot look upon sin with the least degree of allowance (D&C 1:31), *as we become more like Him, neither can we*. The best people have a heightened awareness of what little of the worst is still in them."[9]

Nephi also came unto Jesus seeking a lightening of his burden: "O Lord, wilt thou redeem my soul? Wilt thou deliver me out of the hands of mine enemies? Wilt thou make me that I may shake at the appearance of sin? May the gates of hell be shut continually before me, because that my heart is broken and my spirit is contrite! O Lord, wilt thou not shut the gates of thy righteousness before me, that I may walk in the path of the low valley, that I may be strict in the plain road! O Lord, wilt thou encircle me around in the robe of thy righteousness! O Lord, wilt thou make a way for mine escape before mine enemies! . . . O Lord, I have trusted in thee, and I will trust in thee forever. . . . Yea, I know that God will give liberally to him that asketh. Yea, my God will give me, if I ask not amiss; therefore I will lift up my voice unto thee; yea, I will cry unto thee, my God, the rock of my righteousness. Behold, my voice shall forever ascend up unto thee, my rock and mine everlasting God" (2 Nephi 4:31–35). Even a righteous man such as Nephi carried burdens from sin, which the Lord was able to ease when Nephi came unto him heavy laden.

A modern example of a Nephi-like, righteous person who recognized the burden of sin was President Spencer W. Kimball. When he received his call to become an apostle, he sought solitude in the hills:

"I was accusing myself, and condemning myself and upbraiding myself. I was praying aloud for special blessings from the Lord. I was telling Him that I had not asked for this position, that I was incapable of doing the work, that I was imperfect and weak and human, that I was unworthy of so noble a calling, though I had tried hard and my heart had been right. I knew that I must have been at least partly responsible for offenses and misunderstandings which a few people fancied they had suffered at my hands. I realized that I had been petty and small many times. I did not spare myself. . . . Never had I prayed before as I now prayed. What I wanted and felt I must have was an assurance that I was acceptable to the Lord. I told Him that I neither wanted nor was worthy of a vision or appearance of angels or any special manifestation. I wanted only the calm peaceful assurance that my offering was accepted. Never before had I been tortured as I was now being tortured. . . . Was it a dream which came to me? I was weary and I think I went to sleep for a little. It seemed that in a dream I saw my grandfather and became conscious of the great work he had done. I cannot say that it was a vision, but I do know that with this new experience came a calm like the dying wind, the quieting wave after the storm is passed. I got up, walked to the rocky point and sat on the . . . ledge. My tears were dry, my soul was at peace. A calm feeling of assurance came over me, doubt and questionings subdued. It was as though a great burden had been lifted. I sat in tranquil silence surveying the beautiful valley, thanking the Lord for the satisfaction and the reassuring answer to my prayers. Long I meditated here in peaceful quietude, apart, and I felt nearer my Lord than ever at any time in my life."[10]

In the discussion thus far we have concentrated on how our burdens can become lighter as we come unto Christ. But Jesus does not specifically teach in Matthew 11:29–30 that our burdens will be light; rather he teaches, "Take my yoke upon you, and learn of me . . . for . . . *my burden* is light" (emphasis added). Although they are very much a part of us, the burdens we experience do not belong to us. Jesus redeems us through his Atonement, which means that he has bought and paid for us. As Paul taught the Corinthians: "What? Know ye not that . . . ye are not your own? For ye are bought with a price" (1 Corinthians

6:19–20). In redeeming us, Christ has not only bought us, or our sins, but has also bought our burdens. They belong to him, so we must not try to hang on to them. It is only as we turn them over to him that he can lighten our burdens. In inviting us to come unto him, Jesus is asking us to hand our burdens over to him. Just as he did for Limhi and his people, he will lighten our burdens by removing them from us.

CONCLUSION

$\mathcal{W}$E LIVE IN A WORLD OF EXPECTATIONS. WE HAVE EXPECTA-
tions from employers, spouses, children, friends, communities,
and God. In Matthew's Gospel we find constant teachings about
what Jesus expects from his disciples. Matthew's report of the
Savior's ministry emphasizes works-righteousness, which, as we
have said, are the things we must do to gain salvation. These
expectations are focused to a large extent in the Sermon on the
Mount and include such commandments as the following: "Let
your light so shine before men, that they may see your good
works, and glorify your Father which is in heaven" (Matthew
5:16). "For I say unto you, That except your righteousness shall
exceed the righteousness of the scribes and Pharisees, ye shall in
no case enter into the kingdom of heaven" (5:20). "But I say unto
you, That whosoever is angry with his brother without a cause

shall be in danger of the judgment" (5:22). "Be ye therefore perfect, even as your Father which is in heaven is perfect" (5:48). "Judge not, that ye be not judged" (7:1). "Therefore all things whatsoever ye would that men should do to you, do ye even so to them: for this is the law and the prophets" (7:12).

As Elder Dallin H. Oaks notes, "Most of us have more things expected of us than we can possibly do."[1] If we're not careful we, like Martha, could get to the point where we are "cumbered about much serving" (Luke 10:40). How is it possible to juggle all these religious expectations when our lives are already filled to the brim?

In Matthew's world of expectations, is there any room for the grace that is so prevalent in the writings of Paul? Although the word *grace* (Greek, *charis*) is not found in Matthew's Gospel, it is certainly assumed. We suggest that Matthew 11:28–30 serves as a counterbalance to these expectations and is, in effect, Matthew's equivalent of grace. Jesus' teachings in Matthew on the cost of discipleship, which are real and important to understand and appreciate, are tempered by his promises of rest, an easy yoke, and a light burden. Being one of Jesus' disciples is not what makes life difficult; living in a mortal world is what makes it difficult! Jesus' call to come unto him is a call for us to let him guide us, help us, and comfort us as we struggle with the burdens of mortality. The question that each of us must ask ourselves is, how will we respond to his invitation? We are the chickens that Jesus wants to gather under his wings. In the 3 Nephi account, Jesus reminds all of us that he has in the past, he is now, and he will in the future extend his invitation to us to come unto him (3 Nephi 10:4–6). How we have responded in the past is behind us; what is important is how we choose to respond now and in the future.

Choosing to come unto Jesus and become his disciples does not free us from the burdens of mortality. As Sister Chieko Okazaki explains, "Sometimes we feel that we should not have burdens—that there is something wrong with us if we have problems in our lives. That is not the case. Burdens are part of life, and we all struggle with burdens . . . and there is nothing wicked in the struggle."[2]

The Savior offers his yoke to us to ease the burdens of mortality and to help us achieve eternal glory with him in the kingdom of his Father. He wants to help us because he loves us. President Gordon B. Hinckley taught: "When all else fails, our Lord is there to help us. He has said, 'Come unto me, all ye that labour and are heavy laden, and I will give you rest' (Matthew 11:28). Each of you has burdens. Let the Lord help you in carrying those burdens. Again He has said, 'Take my yoke upon you, . . . for my yoke is easy, and my burden is light' (Matthew 11:29–30). He stands ready to help—to help each of us—with every burden. He loves us so much that He shed drops of blood in Gethsemane, then permitted evil and wicked men to take Him, to compel Him to carry the cross to Golgotha, to suffer beyond any power of description terrible pain when He was nailed to the cross, to be lifted up on the cross, and to die for each of us. He was the one perfect man, without blemish, to walk the earth. He was the Savior and Redeemer of mankind. Because of His sacrifice, because of His

Atonement, all of us will at some time arise in the Resurrection, and beyond that there will be marvelous opportunities to go forward on the road of immortality and eternal life."[3]

We testify also that the Savior's gracious entreaty to come unto him is a demonstration of his love and concern for our individual earthly needs as well as our hope for eternal life in his presence. When we come unto him as true disciples, he will extend to us the grace and mercy that only he can give, eagerly embracing us in his loving arms, easing whatever pains and burdens we bear, and gently distilling upon our souls the rest he has promised to those who follow him. Although his magnificent Atonement may seem virtually incomprehensible to us now, we can be sure that his perfect sacrifice, offered because he loves us perfectly, will easily bridge the gap between who we are today and who we can become as his disciples. As we learn of him, serve him, and willingly take up his cross, the reality of his rest—that perfect assurance of relief and divine sustenance—will be ours to enjoy both here and hereafter.

NOTES

INTRODUCTION

1. Henry B. Eyring, "Come unto Christ," *Ensign*, March 2008, 49.

2. Jeffrey R. Holland, *Trusting Jesus* (Salt Lake City: Deseret Book, 2003), 84.

3. Mark Allan Powell, *Introducing the New Testament: A Historical, Literary, and Theological Survey* (Grand Rapids, Mich.: Baker Academic, 2009), 123.

4. See Terryl L. Givens, *People of Paradox: A History of Mormon Culture* (New York: Oxford University Press, 2007), 26.

5. Dallin H. Oaks, *His Holy Name* (Salt Lake City: Deseret Book, 2009), 75.

6. Bruce C. Hafen, *Spiritually Anchored in Unsettled Times* (Salt Lake City: Deseret Book, 2009), 16.

7. Neil L. Andersen, "'Repent . . . That I May Heal You,'" *Ensign*, November 2009, 40–41.

8. Neal A. Maxwell, "Willing to Submit," *Ensign*, May 1985, 71.

9. Dietrich Bonhoeffer, *The Cost of Discipleship* (New York: Simon & Schuster, 1995), 61.

10. Henry B. Eyring, "Home for Christmas," *Ensign*, December 2009, 6.

11. Chieko N. Okazaki, *Lighten Up!* (Salt Lake City: Deseret Book, 1993), 173.

12. Neal A. Maxwell, *If Thou Endure It Well* (Salt Lake City: Bookcraft, 1996), 114.

13. Hafen, *Spiritually Anchored*, 3–4.

14. See Craig Harline, *Sunday: A History of the First Day from Babylonia to the Super Bowl* (New York: Doubleday, 2007), 216–18.

15. Boyd K. Packer, *Let Not Your Hearts Be Troubled* (Salt Lake City: Bookcraft, 1991), 181.

16. Spencer W. Kimball, in Conference Report, April 1974, 184.

17. Tad R. Callister, *The Infinite Atonement* (Salt Lake City: Deseret Book, 2000), 196.

18. Raymond E. Brown, *An Introduction to the New Testament* (New York: Doubleday, 1997), 184.

19. See Givens, *People of Paradox*, xiv.

20. See Richard Neitzel Holzapfel and Kent P. Jackson, "To the Least, the Last, and the Lost," in *To Save the Lost: An Easter Celebration* (Provo: Religious Studies Center, Brigham Young University, 2009), vi–xi.

21. Hafen, *Spiritually Anchored*, 4–5.

22. Hafen, *Spiritually Anchored*, 10–11.

23. A. E. Harvey, *The New English Bible Companion to the New Testament* (New York: Oxford University Press, 1979), 56.

Chapter 1: Jesus' Invitation and Promise

1. A. M. Hunter, "Crux Criticorum—Matt. XI.25–30—A Re-Appraisal," *New Testament Studies* 8 (1962): 241.

2. James E. Talmage, *Jesus the Christ* (Salt Lake City: Deseret Book, 1982), 242.

3. John W. Welch, "A Masterpiece: Alma 36," *Rediscovering the Book of Mormon*, ed. John L. Sorenson and Melvin J. Thorne (Provo, Utah: Foundation for Ancient Research and Mormon Studies; Salt Lake City: Deseret Book, 1991), 114.

4. See April De Conick, "The Yoke Saying in the Gospel of Thomas 90," *Vigiliae Christianae* 44, no. 3 (1990): 280.

CHAPTER 2: KNOWING THE FATHER

1. See Richard Neitzel Holzapfel, Dana M. Pike, and David Rolph Seely, *Jehovah and the World of the Old Testament: An Illustrated Reference for Latter-day Saints* (Salt Lake City: Deseret Book, 2009), 379.

2. All references to the Joseph Smith Translation are from Thomas A. Wayment, ed., *The Complete Joseph Smith Translation of the New Testament: A Side-by-Side Comparison with the King James Version* (Salt Lake City: Deseret Book, 2005).

3. Ben Witherington III, *Smyth & Helwys Bible Commentary: Matthew* (Macon, Ga.: Smyth & Helwys, 2006), 237.

4. Bruce J. Malina and Richard L. Rohrbaugh, *Social Science Commentary on the Synoptic Gospels* (Minneapolis, Minn.: Fortress Press, 1992), 94.

5. As cited in James D. G. Dunn, *Jesus Remembered* (Grand Rapids, Minn.: Eerdmans, 2003), 719.

6. N. T. Wright, *Matthew for Everyone, Part 1, Chapters 1–15* (Louisville, Ky.: SPCK, Westminster John Knox Press, 2004), 137.

CHAPTER 3: JESUS' AUTHORITY

1. See Richard Neitzel Holzapfel, Dana M. Pike, and David Rolph Seely, *Jehovah and the World of the Old Testament: An Illustrated*

Reference for Latter-day Saints (Salt Lake City: Deseret Book, 2009), 379.

2. See S. Kent Brown and Richard Neitzel Holzapfel, *The Lost 500 Years: What Happened between the Old and New Testaments* (Salt Lake City: Deseret Book, 2006), 38–47.

3. See Brown and Holzapfel, *Lost 500 Years*, 98.

4. Brown and Holzapfel, *Lost 500 Years*, 160.

5. Benedict T. Viviano, "The Gospel of Matthew," in Raymond E. Brown, Joseph A. Fitzmyer, and Roland E. Murphy, eds., *The New Jerome Biblical Commentary* (Englewood Cliffs, N.J.: Prentice Hall, 1990), 653.

6. Daniel Sinclair, "Oral Law," in R. J. Zwi Werblowsky and Geoffrey Wigoder, eds., *The Oxford Dictionary of the Jewish Religion* (New York: Oxford University Press, 1997), 512.

7. See Brown and Holzapfel, *Lost 500 Years*, 120–26.

8. See Brown and Holzapfel, *Lost 500 Years*, 134–44.

9. A. E. Harvey, *The New English Bible Companion to the New Testament* (New York: Oxford University Press, 1979), 55.

10. Bruce C. Hafen, *Spiritually Anchored in Unsettled Times* (Salt Lake City: Deseret Book, 2009), 20–21.

Chapter 4: A Call to Discipleship

1. Michael J. Wilkins, *Discipleship in the Ancient World and Matthew's Gospel*, 2d ed. (Grand Rapids, Mich.: Baker Books, 1995), 221.

2. Wilkins, *Discipleship in the Ancient World*, 221–22.

3. He uses it thirteen times in his Gospel: 4:23; 5:2, 19; 7:29; 9:35; 11:1; 13:54; 15:9; 21:23; 22:16; 26:55; 28:15; 28:20.

4. Günther Bornkamm, "The Stilling of the Storm in Matthew," in *Tradition and Interpretation in Matthew*, ed. Günther Bornkamm, Gerhard Barth, and Heinz Joachim Held, trans. Percy Scott (Philadelphia: Westminster, 1963), 52–57.

5. W. D. Davies and Dale C. Allison, *A Critical and Exegetical Commentary on the Gospel according to Saint Matthew*, 3 vols. (Edinburgh: T&T Clark, 1991), 2:681.

6. James E. Faust, "The Price of Discipleship," *Ensign*, April 1999, 4.

7. *Deute* serves as the plural of *deuro*, which we will see used in the invitation to the rich young man, s.v. δεῦρο. Frederick William Danker, ed., *A Greek-English Lexicon of the New Testament and Other Early Christian Literature*, 3d ed. (Chicago: University of Chicago Press, 2000), 176.

8. Jeffrey R. Holland, "Broken Things to Mend," *Ensign*, May 2006, 69.

9. Neal A. Maxwell, "'Swallowed Up in the Will of the Father,'" *Ensign*, November 1995, 24.

CHAPTER 5: REST

1. Joseph Fielding Smith, *The Way to Perfection* (Salt Lake City: Deseret Book, 1984), 149.

2. Neal A. Maxwell, "'Brightness of Hope,'" *Ensign*, November 1994, 35.

3. See s.v. σπουδάζω in Frederick William Danker, ed., *A Greek-English Lexicon of the New Testament and Other Early Christian Literature*, 3d ed. (Chicago: University of Chicago Press, 2000), 763.

4. See Stephen E. Robinson, *Believing Christ: The Parable of the Bicycle and Other Good News* (Salt Lake City: Deseret Book, 1992), 11.

5. James E. Faust, "The Lord's Day," *Ensign*, November 1991, 34.

6. Lucy Mack Smith, *History of Joseph Smith by His Mother*, ed. Preston Nibley (Salt Lake City: Bookcraft, 1979), 324.

7. Joseph F. Smith, *Gospel Doctrine* (Salt Lake City: Deseret Book, 1986), 58.

8. Smith, *Gospel Doctrine*, 126.

Chapter 6: An Easy Yoke

1. Charles L. Tyer, "Yoke," in *The Anchor Bible Dictionary*, ed. David Noel Freedman (New York: Doubleday, 1992), 6:1026.

2. Mishnah, Aboth 3.5; cited in Herbert Danby, ed., *The Mishnah* (London: Oxford University Press, 1950), 450.

3. See Tyer, "Yoke," 6:1027.

4. Fulton J. Sheen, quoted in D. Todd Christofferson, "Moral Discipline," *Ensign*, November 2009, 106.

5. Bruce C. Hafen, *Spiritually Anchored in Unsettled Times* (Salt Lake City: Deseret Book, 2009), 12.

6. Neal A. Maxwell, "'Swallowed Up in the Will of the Father,'" *Ensign*, November 1995, 24.

7. Neal A. Maxwell, General Authority Training Meeting, April 2004; cited in Hafen, *Spiritually Anchored*, 23.

8. Hafen, *Spiritually Anchored*, 27.

9. Ben Witherington III, *Smyth & Helwys Bible Commentary: Matthew* (Macon, Ga.: Smyth & Helwys, 2006), 244.

10. Neal A. Maxwell, *Men and Women of Christ* (Salt Lake City: Bookcraft, 1991), 103.

11. Neal A. Maxwell, *Meek and Lowly* (Salt Lake City: Bookcraft, 1987), 5–6.

12. Thomas S. Monson, "The Master Bridge Builder," *Ensign*, January 2008, 6.

13. Jeffrey R. Holland, "Broken Things to Mend," *Ensign*, May 2006, 69.

14. Neal A. Maxwell, "Jesus, the Perfect Mentor," *Ensign*, February 2001, 13.

15. Neal A. Maxwell, *The Neal A. Maxwell Quote Book*, ed. Cory H. Maxwell, illustrated ed. (Salt Lake City: Deseret Book, 2009), 204.

16. M. Russell Ballard, "O Be Wise," *Ensign*, November 2006, 19.

CHAPTER 7: A LIGHT BURDEN

1. John Nolland, *The Gospel of Matthew: A Commentary on the Greek Text* (Grand Rapids, Mich.: Eerdmans, 2005), 478.

2. Thomas S. Monson, "Duty Calls," *Ensign*, May 1996, 44.

3. Neal A. Maxwell, "It's Service, Not Status, That Counts," *Ensign*, July 1975, 7.

4. Richard G. Scott, "Trust in the Lord," *Ensign*, November 1995, 16.

5. Jeffrey R. Holland, "The Inconvenient Messiah," *Ensign*, February 1984, 70.

6. Gordon B. Hinckley, "Be Not Faithless," *Ensign*, April 1989, 4.

7. Dallin H. Oaks, "He Heals the Heavy Laden," *Ensign*, November 2006, 8.

8. Oaks, "He Heals the Heavy Laden," 8.

9. Neal A. Maxwell, *Notwithstanding My Weakness* (Salt Lake City: Deseret Book, 1981), 16–17; emphasis in original.

10. Edward L. Kimball and Andrew E. Kimball, Jr., *Spencer W. Kimball: Twelfth President of The Church of Jesus Christ of Latter-day Saints* (Salt Lake City: Bookcraft, 1977), 193–95.

CONCLUSION

1. Dallin H. Oaks, "Good, Better, Best," *Ensign*, November 2007, 104.

2. Chieko N. Okazaki, "Finding Lightness in Our Burdens," in *Women Steadfast in Christ*, ed. Dawn Hall Anderson and Marie Cornwall (Salt Lake City: Deseret Book, 1992), 205.

3. Gordon B. Hinckley, "Stand True and Faithful," *Ensign*, May 1996, 94.

INDEX

public disapproval, 34; of false
traditions and values, 35; of
law of Moses, 51; of the effects
of sin, 52–54; meaning of, 81;
are lifted in many ways, 82–83;
of Pharisaical interpretation,
84; Jesus will make, light, 86;
faith will make, light, 87; God
converses through, 92; Nephi
seeks lightening of his, 97–98;
are bought by Jesus, 100; are part
of life, 103

Callister, Tad R., on the Atonement,
12
"Cease, or stop," meaning of, 64
Change, 4
Chiasmus, 16
Christofferson, Todd D., on rejecting
Christ's easy yoke, 75
Consumption, unrestricted, 34
Come unto Christ: an invitation, 1;
everyone invited to, 8; as call to
discipleship, 47–48; as crucial
key, 55
Commandments: of men rejected by
Jesus, 29; living, definition of, 46

Deuro, "come," 48
Deute, "come," 47
Didaskō, "teaching in general," 38
Dikaiosynē, "righteousness," 16
Disciples: Christ's commission to,
38; as students, 39; faith of,
42; consecrate what is most
important, 45; are not distracted,

46; calling of Peter, James, and
John as, 47–48
Discipleship: halfhearted manner
of, 4–6; through works-
righteousness, 16; Matthew's
Gospel as discourses on, 37–38;
commitment of, 39; as knowing
Christ through experience, 42;
as doing what is right, 44; as
conscious decision, 46; as call to
minister to others, 48; costs of,
50, 85
Distractions, 9

Epignōsis, "experiential knowledge,"
40–41
Emotion, Matthew 11:28–30 as
spiritual, 15
Entitlement, personal, 34
Essenes, discredit temple, 28
Eyring, Henry B.: on an invitation
to come to Christ, 1; on
forgiveness, 5

Faith, 42, 69
"Father," meaning of, 29
Fall, the, consequences of, 88
Fast offering, 10
Faust, James E.: on price of
discipleship, 46; on Sabbath, 64
Fishers of men, story of becoming, 47
Forgiveness: sweetness of divine,
4; of halfhearted disciples, 5; of
man with palsy, 52; for those
who repent, 80
Fortion, "burden is light," 81

INDEX

INDEX

Sabbath as day of, 64; as end of mortal struggles, 67; no physical, in Church, 69; as perfect assurance of relief and divine sustenance, 104

Repentance, obtaining through Atonement, 63

Revelation: necessary to know who Jesus is, 43; personal, of Lucy Mack Smith, 66–67; personal, can bring rest, 70

Rich young man, story of, 48

Righteousness, 16

Robinson, Stephen E., on believing Christ, 62

Sabbath: Jesus as Lord of, 17; Jesus with authority over, 19; story of Jesus and Sabbath day, 25–26; observance of, separated Jews from Gentiles, 26–27; examples of work forbidden on, 28; overriding Torah interpretation of, 29; provides freedom, 30; story of healing on, 31–32; a day to do good, 32; strict observance of, 33; appropriately observing, 64; as sign of the covenant, 65

Sacrifice, complete 56

Samaritans, rejected temple, 28

Satan, knows scripture, 30

Scott, Richard G., on two reasons for adversity, 91

Scriptures, knowing without understanding, 30

Selfishness: as failure to share abundance, 10; self-denial as form of, 11

Sermon on the Mount, 40, 49, 101

Shabbat, "to cease, or to stop," 64

Sheen, Fulton J., on failing to accept yoke of Christ, 75

Simon the Pharisee, 53–54

Sin: effects of, may be subtle, 52; as debilitating, 54; all have committed, 96

Smith, Hyrum, death of, 66

Smith, Joseph, Jr.: death of, 66; in Liberty Jail, 70–71

Smith, Joseph F., on entering into God's rest, 69

Smith, Joseph Fielding, on membership in Church not being for the idler, 57

Smith, Lucy Mack, on her sons receiving rest in the Lord, 66–67

Sower, parable of, 2

Spoudazō, "zealous, or eager, make every effort," 62

Stories: of Jesus and Sabbath day, 25–26; of asking Jesus if it was lawful to heal on the Sabbath, 31–32; of Peter, Andrew, James and John to become fishers of men, 47; of rich young man, 48; of woman anointing Jesus, 53–54; of Lucy Mack Smith, 66–67; of Joseph in Liberty Jail, 71; of Alma and Limhi, 82–83; of Adam and Eve, 88; of Job, 89–92; of Alma the Younger, 93–94; of Nephi seeking a lightening of his burden, 97–98; of Spencer W.

117